PRAISE FOR

Career Coaching Your Kids

*T*HE AUTHORS COACH PARENTS *in ways of stimu-lating their children's career exploration, at the same time parents are keeping their distance to allow childhood creativity to flourish. The book thus strikes a very sensible balance between parental involvement and hands-off-ness. I like the book's sensitivity to the nuances of parent-child interaction. It provides a wealth of useful and supportive guidelines for parents to follow.*

Howard Figler, Ph.D.
author, *The Complete Job-Search Handbook*

*H*OW I WISH *I could have had this career planning when I was young," is the lament from my adult clients in career transition. Reading this book is an absolute must for parents and teachers.*

Helen Harkness, Ph.D.
CEO, Career Design Associates, Inc.
author, *The Career Chase* and
Don't Stop the Career Clock

*A*N EXCELLENT AND PRACTICAL GUIDE *for parents and other adults helping young people through the maze of career decisions. This book is truly an invaluable resource for anyone working with children, adolescents, and young adults!*

Anne Kingan, MAT
career coach and
educational consultant
president, AK Consulting Services

CAREER COACHING YOUR KIDS

CAREER COACHING YOUR KIDS

GUIDING YOUR CHILD THROUGH THE PROCESS OF CAREER DISCOVERY

Second Edition

David H. Montross

Theresa E. Kane

Robert J. Ginn, Jr.

Davies-Black Publishing

Palo Alto, California

Published by Davies-Black Publishing, a division of CPP, Inc., 3803 East Bayshore Road, Palo Alto, CA 94303; 800-624-1765.

Special discounts on bulk quantities of Davies-Black books are available to corporations, professional associations, and other organizations. For details, contact the Director of Marketing and Sales at Davies-Black Publishing; 650-691-9123; fax 650-623-9271.

Visit the Davies-Black Publishing web site at www.daviesblack.com.

08 07 06 05 04   10 9 8 7 6 5 4 3 2 1
Printed in the United States of America

Library of Congress Cataloging-in-Publication Data
Montross, David H.
    Career coaching your kids : guiding your child through the process of
career discovery / David H. Montross, Theresa E. Kane, Robert J. Ginn, Jr.—2nd ed.
        p. cm.
    Includes bibliographical references and index.
    ISBN 0-89106-182-7 (pbk.)
    1. Vocational guidance. 2. Youth—Employment.
  I. Kane, Theresa E., II. Ginn, Jr., Robert Jay III. Title.
  HF5381.M64 2004
  331.702—dc22

                                                      2003024684

SECOND EDITION
First printing 2004

DEDICATED TO OUR PARENTS

CONTENTS

PREFACE TO THE SECOND EDITION

WHEN WE DECIDED TO WRITE the first edition of *Career Coaching Your Kids*, we believed there was a compelling need for it. Now, not only are we more certain that the need exists, but we are convinced it has grown. The number of jobs available has decreased markedly, making a well-thought-out career plan more important than ever. Interesting and challenging jobs at the beginning of a career can open doors in the future, and those interesting and challenging jobs will go to those who know what they want and have done some preparation.

Since the first edition was published, we have met with career development professionals and parents who attended workshops we developed based on the ideas contained in the book. We have met with parents of high school students and of students about to graduate from college. We have had important dialogues with high school guidance counselors and college career planning professionals, about both their coaching challenges and their frustration with how to help parents take a more active and helpful role. We have given presentations to professionals in a variety of fields. With all of these audiences, we found receptivity to and acceptance of our thesis that parents influence their children's career discovery process, and that they need assistance to do so constructively, and we encountered interesting challenges to some of our core ideas that forced us to expand our thinking and perspectives.

Soon after our first edition was published, new psychological literature confirmed our concerns about the impact parental overinvolvement can have on a person's career decisions. Children who follow paths they think their parents want them to follow, instead of discovering for themselves who they can become, can experience long-term frustration and job dissatisfaction. As Mary Jacobsen (1999) noted in her book *Hand-Me-Down Dreams*, hand-me-downs may serve a functional purpose, but they are most often not what we would choose as our own. Too many children go in the direction they are led, willingly or not. At the same time we met many parents who had adopted a hands-off approach that left them frustrated by their children's indecision. Our model of appropriate levels of parental involvement was upheld.

Unfortunately, our experiences also reinforced our belief that many high school and college students have limited access to high-quality career services. Overworked high school counselors are forced to focus on many other problems young people face today, with career planning ranking low on the list of priorities. While there were certainly many encouraging exceptions, and some select state education systems that have placed a high priority on career education, parents overall cannot assume that this important aspect of their child's life is being properly and adequately attended to by the child's guidance counselor. With rising tuition costs, parents and children cannot afford to make haphazard last-minute choices about the direction they plan to head, or even make assumptions that college is the only appropriate choice.

Finally, an observation that led to some of the additions to this edition: While the majority of resources (books, workbooks, videos, etc.) in 1997 were geared toward high school and college-age students, with few available for parents, a review of the popular literature in 2003 revealed a dramatic increase in resources for middle school and, to a lesser extent, elementary school students. This was an encouraging sign that people are recognizing that career decision making should not begin in junior and senior high school. Yet there are still few resources available for parents, most drafted by high school counselors as part of their career curricula, and very few that help younger children open up their imaginations about work roles.

So we are pleased to be able to offer you this second edition, with a much-expanded summary and resource section and new ideas to consider as you continue down this important path. We hope you find this edition helpful, and as always we welcome your comments and reactions. If we have learned anything, it is that everyone has his or her own story to tell on this topic, and it is the richness of the stories we hear that informs and encourages us.

PREFACE TO THE FIRST EDITION

EDUCATIONAL PSYCHOLOGIST Brian Costello summed up the dilemma and key questions we will address in this book: From the day their children are born, most parents have dreams of who those children will become. Parents may want their sons and daughters to have everything they never had or want them to choose a career that they view as providing security. But when do parents lose sight of what the children themselves want and need from life? How can parents help their children become aware of and realize their own career aspirations?

Research continues to suggest that career decision making is one of the major challenges young people face and that parents need help in helping their child choose a career path

(Otto 1996). Despite a general perception that children listen to everyone but their parents, children of all ages in fact continue to look to parents as role models and advisors. A survey by the National Association of Colleges and Employers (1996) confirmed that career choices are most heavily influenced by parents. Yet few resources are available to help parents understand and fulfill their roles in their children's career decision making process.

WHY WE WROTE THIS BOOK

As career counselors, we believe that there are career decision–making processes that successfully lead people—young and old—to career satisfaction. As educators, researchers, parents, and adults with career histories, we also believe there are appropriate and inappropriate roles that parents can play that will help or hinder their child's career decision making journey. Our collective experience includes college-level counseling at Harvard University and Holy Cross College; career outplacement and counseling at major corporations, including Digital Equipment Corporation and Norton Company; and community career services work with local high school students, administrators, guidance counselors, and parents.

Although bookshelves are crowded with guidelines for working adults, managers, and new college graduates, little is available to address the needs of children and parents as integral influences on each other's career decisions. Yet research indicates that parents play a critical role in children's career development. We have seen the consequences of inattention to how careers are discussed with children and young adults, and we believe a guidebook such as this is an important addition to existing career planning literature. It is written primarily for parents but will interest all educators, career and guidance counselors, and caretakers such as aunts, uncles, and grandparents.

This book goes beyond college guidance and occupational information to address the entire process of career assessment, exploration, and action planning necessary for you to help your children find work that fits their skills, interests, personality, and developmental needs. We believe career planning, like parenting, is a lifelong process, and therefore we discuss the career planning process, and the roles a parent plays in it, from a full life-span perspective, birth to adulthood. We begin with what we believe is a critical step for you to consider before thinking about helping your children with their career decisions: assessing your own career decisions and how your own parents influenced them. This will introduce you to the career planning process we recommend and give you a context within which to explore the messages you are currently giving your children about work.

Career decision making begins when there are only inklings of what we might become.

Aristotle thought that humans follow a growth pattern he called *entelechy*—becoming what you already are. When you look at a seed, you see no resemblance to the flower it can become if carefully planted and supported in growth. Yet Aristotle knew from experience that the seed possesses the potential, the *entelechy*, of the flower even though there is no outward similarity. Career decision making begins with trying to understand our potential in the early stages of development, when there are only inklings of what we might become. The challenge for parents is to spot the signs of a vocation in the early stages of its growth before it is exhibited. Perhaps more important in terms of your involvement in your child's career decisions, the challenge is to refrain from manufacturing ambitions and potential that may not naturally be there.

PARENTAL RESPONSIBILITY IN CAREER COACHING

This book encourages you to help your children make decisions for themselves. You can rely on experts in schools and professional assessment specialists to help you identify the talents and potential that emerge in the early stages of your child's growth (see Parent Tool Kit section for resource suggestions). But your task is to help your child learn how to make decisions consistent with her deepest, wisest self. We define *child* as anyone from an imaginative preschooler pretending to be a doctor to an adult child coming to you for support after having been downsized out of a job.

Decision-making skills are akin to language skills. Like trying to learn a second language in a class as opposed to living in a foreign country and seemingly learning by osmosis, career decision making can be taught by experts but flows more easily when taught at home. Children learn to be concerned or indifferent, to celebrate or to grieve, to reject or to accept largely by imitation and reward in the home, in the neighborhood, and in the school. The foundations of who they become are built by the parent.

A ten-year study (Steinberg 1990) that surveyed 20,000 students in ninth to twelfth grades suggested that parents think there is nothing they can do, that career coaching is the school's job. Yet "even if schools had the resources to meet young people's career guidance needs, neither teachers nor counselors can replace the critical influence parents have on their sons' and daughters' career plans. The parental role in career decisions can be injurious if not understood and handled well, but it is also unavoidable" (Otto 1996; see also Jacobsen, 1998). Sherri Eng (1996) notes that as funding for career services at public schools declines, parents realize they must take on more responsibility for helping their daughters and sons make career decisions.

The challenge is to help your children discover career paths that lead to the fulfillment of their own dreams, that use their natural and developed skills, interests, and values to their fullest potential. At the same time, they need your advice and resources to help them make informed and constructive choices amid a wide range of diverse options. You can do this by working through some of the exercises and advice in this book with your child; forming partnerships with his or her school guidance office; helping to identify resources (such as career counselors, assessment centers, and sources of job information); and showing genuine but non-coercive interest.

PURPOSE AND ORGANIZATION

The purpose of this book is to provide a comprehensive career decision–making guide for parents of children, adolescents, and young adults. We offer professional advice on the specific roles that you as a parent can play during various stages of your child's development and during predictable steps in the career decision–making cycle. We conclude with an outline of resources available to parents.

Part One (Chapters 1–3) provides an opportunity to reflect on your own experiences and career satisfaction and to consider other parental roles you play. We encourage you to think about how to balance imposing too much parental influence on your child's career decision with the need to play an active and supportive role throughout the process. Part Two (Chapters 4–7) provides a comprehensive career decision–making process, a framework to help your children explore career options. The focus is on how you can help them work through each step. Part Three (Chapters 8–10) provides an overview of key events in the lives of children, adolescents, and young adults that may influence their career decision–making needs. The Parent Tool Kit section provides an up-to-date listing of career planning resources for children, as well as for parents and educators.

CONSEQUENCES

We believe there are potentially serious consequences to not paying proper attention to this important parental responsibility. You may overinfluence your child to follow *your* dreams and not *theirs*, which may cause psychological difficulties later in life. Other consequences are of a more practical nature: If you are paying rising educational expenses, you want this substantial investment to be made toward the development of skills and qualities that lead to your child's satisfaction. Education is rarely a waste of time, but most parents cannot afford to extend or repeat the funding of college expenses when their child decides to head in a different career direction.

As parent, you play a critical role throughout your child's life and career. How your role changes and how you fulfill it are the foundations of this book. Above all, you are one of the most influential role models your children have. You can overdo advice by steering them in directions you want them to go, or, through the guidance offered in this book, you can help them define the direction that feels right to *them*. We hope to support you as you support your children through the ups and downs of the working world.

ACKNOWLEDGMENTS

Many people provided input and ideas for this book. We want to thank the following people who were especially helpful to us:

Victoria Ball, Brown University; JoAnn Bowlsby-Harris, American College Testing; Gillian Davies, parent; Ned Dunbar, educational consultant; Robert Elland, career counselor; Ann Flynn, Ph.D., Holy Cross College; Carol Ann Hamilton, Clinton High School, guidance counselor; Natalie Jangl, Tantasqua High School, guidance counselor; Anne Kingan, career and academic coach; Charlotte Klarr, educational consultant; Virginia Moore, National Career Development Association; Judy Rogers, parent and educator; Pat Welsh, Longmeadow High School, guidance counselor.

PART ONE

BRIDGING CAREERS

BETWEEN PARENT AND CHILD

EFORE DELVING INTO THE TASK of helping your children with the career discovery process, you need to build a foundation on which to develop and enhance your role as parental career coach. The intent of this book is to give you a framework and process for discussing career options with your kids. We begin by giving you the opportunity to step back, before you engage with your children, to apply the career decision framework to your own experience.

In Chapter 1, "What Is Career Coaching?" we clarify what this journey you are about to experience is and is not. We look at the benefits of career coaching, and we share some current research on what help students want from their parents. These findings suggest a significant difference between how parents and their children perceive parental career advice. We pose an essential question, Whose career is it? and propose that finding that fine line between underinvolvement and overinvolvement in your child's career decisions is one of the most important and difficult aspects of successful career coaching. We position the career coaching role within a holistic framework, acknowledging and integrating it with the complex, multidimensional relationship that you have with your child. We review some fundamental parenting skills, applicable to all situations, which will bring you a long way toward being an effective career coach.

In Chapter 2, we provide questions and tools for you to explore your own career history and what it has taught you. We introduce the career decision model and encourage you to apply it to your own career decisions, both in the past and in your current work situation. We examine important foundational questions for you to consider before working with your children, including asking you to think about who influenced your career and the role your parents played.

In Chapter 3, we contemplate how the world of work today differs from the workplace you and your parents entered and how it will differ from the workplace of the next generation. We outline some general trends, along with suggestions for how to help your children explore opportunities and develop the skills that will help them succeed regardless of the occupation they choose. Finally, we discuss the complexity of changing occupational trends and offer ways in which to access the information your children will need as they move forward in the career decision–making process.

Though you may be anxious to move on and begin the process with your children (and thereby tempted to skip over this chapter, which focuses on you), we encourage you to take the time to build this foundation of understanding first. Try out the model by applying it to what you know best. Think back and learn from your own experiences while acknowledging that some of your lessons may no longer be appropriate in the occupational world your child is about to join. We believe this preliminary work will strengthen your ability to work with the career decision model and will make you a more effective career coach. You just may also discover ways to enhance your own career satisfaction along the way!

1

WHAT IS CAREER COACHING?

S AN ICEBREAKER EXERCISE at the beginning of our career planning workshop for adults, we ask participants how, at age six, they answered the question, What do you want to be when you grow up? Most of us can think of areas of interest in our early years, and many of us realize that our aspirations were aligned with role models in our lives at the time (teaching is a popular aspiration for first-graders). Our next question is how those aspirations match what the participant is doing today. In rare cases, someone says, "I knew I wanted to be an engineer when I was six, and I just followed those dreams until I got there." Most laugh when they think about how different their career lives have turned out from what they thought they would be.

Some kids know what they want to do early on and spend their lives moving toward those aspirations. Most, however, struggle with vocational decisions, which have been cited by numerous studies as the top concern of high school students and young adults. Adolescents' search for identity translates in large part to how they will define themselves in terms of the vocational roles they intend to play (Vondracek 1993; Blustein, Devinis, & Kidney 1989; Marcia 1980).

BENEFITS OF CAREER COACHING

Career coaching provides your child with a framework with which to organize his or her thinking about career options and what it would take to get there. Parental career coaching is helping your child develop a career support network, which can also include teachers, guidance counselors, employers, and role models. Career choice plays an important part in people's lives—in their overall life satisfaction as well as their economic security and social status. Coaching provides children with a compass pointed toward their vocational life's journey and destinations.

Beyond specific focus on choices about work, coaching provides parents and children with a tangible way to communicate and stay connected. It gives you the chance to show interest in your children's long-term future and to discover how they view the world and their place in it. In partnership with guidance counselors, teachers, and career specialists, this is an opportunity to give your children hope in the future and motivation to excel. Coaching also gives you the chance to relate to your children in a constructive, nondisciplinary role. Chart 1 shows a sample response to a question your child may ask, and Chart 2 lists the kinds of support students want from their parents. Benefits include helping them understand themselves better; setting them on the right path; and widening their perspective to prepare them for a changing world. In the process, it just might give you time to contemplate the direction your own career is heading.

WHAT CAREER COACHING IS NOT

Career coaching is *not* telling your children what to do with their lives. It is helping them decide what is right for them. It is not an excuse to expound on how things should be or lament how much better or worse they were in your day. Sharing your career journey can help them see how you dealt with your own career decisions, but only within the context of helping them understand how to deal with their own.

Most important, career coaching is not about forcing children to make decisions prematurely without the benefit of experimentation, research, and normal childhood experience. It is not about forcing children to grow up too fast. In fact, as David Elkind notes in *The Hurried Child* (2001), rushing children through natural developmental stages is detrimental, and is not what we condone at all. "Kids should have fun being kids, not anguish over future careers. At fifteen, sixteen, seventeen years old, you don't have to decide what you want to do for the rest of your life" (Eng 1996).

College career counselors Wayne Reschke and Karen Knierim (1987) noted that parents often exert undue pressure on students to make career decisions without the context of the ongoing career coaching framework we are suggesting here:

CHART 1	Q: How can I make decisions now that will affect me for life? Aren't I too young? What if I change my mind?
RESPONSES TO QUESTIONS YOUR CHILD MIGHT ASK	A: Good questions. But remember, you choose the kinds of people you want for friends. You select subjects to study. You determine whether joining clubs or teams is right for you. You choose the college you wish to attend. You elect whether or not to find part-time work. These and other decisions are invaluable reinforcement of your decision-making skills. No decision is irrevocable if you consciously try to make decisions that allow flexibility in the future.

From Joyce Lain Kennedy, *An Age for Decisions*, 1993

"The pressure is often intense, and unrealistic expectations are not uncommon. Parents are well meaning and want the best for their children, but they often express that concern in counterproductive ways. There is increased pressure to not waste time on anything that isn't marketable." These counselors found a significant difference between how parents and their children perceive the career advice parents provide. Although parents in their study indicated a desire not to interfere in their child's career decisions, they also expressed doubt that young people are capable of making such decisions independently. Parents' perceptions that they provide encouragement, moral support, financial support, advice, and contacts can be perceived by children as meddling or pressure to make a living and earn a decent wage. One student confided, "My father makes me make a decision about my future, so I make something up." Some young

CHART 2	**Support:** "They've always been supportive but never pushy."
	Information: "Parents are good for their real-life perspective." "My father is very helpful in alerting me to various professions." "I think that parents could help a student research possibilities."
WHAT HELP DO STUDENTS WANT FROM PARENTS?	**Personal insights:** Parents can be helpful in sorting out career possibilities "because they know me well." "They have been especially supportive just simply by talking over career possibilities and what sort of jobs I might be good at."
	Contacts: "I think that parents could help a student . . . seek out guidance from people they know." Thirty-nine percent saw their parents as being of little or no help in providing contacts for job prospects.
	Motivation: "My parents are helpful in pushing me to decide what I want to do."

Source: "UVA Students Talk About Parents and Career," in Reschke and Knierim, *How Parents Influence Career Choice*, 1987

people found the tension to decide was so intense that they stayed clear of any occupations suggested by their parents, eliminating potentially viable career paths.

There are, however, many age-appropriate actions that parents can take that will facilitate healthy career decisions later in their children's lives. The premise of this book is that there are steps parents can take, and some mistakes they can avoid, that will help their children expand rather than limit their perceptions of career opportunities available to them. Parental career coaching is defined here in a much broader context than sitting down to complete a career planning form or search for a job. "Parents can lay a suitable ground-work for career development of their children by influencing them broadly to become responsible and capable human beings" (Young 1994).

Career coaching is the process of helping your children discover who they are and what interests them, helping them develop imagination, and courage, and belief in their abilities. It is an exciting, ongoing, motivating process, not one that saddles children with static and irreversible decisions.

WHOSE CAREER IS IT?

"I want my kids to have everything I never had." The danger in this well-intentioned, heartfelt sentiment is that what you want them to have may not be what they want. Children need to follow their own dreams based on their unique combination of interests, abilities, and values. For example, if you grew up in poverty, your wish for your children may be that they get a "good job" so that they earn a good living and are able to purchase a nice home in the suburbs. But your child may want to do volunteer work in a third-world country to help those less fortunate.

Or you may have worked hard all your life for material things and feel strongly that the stress of the rat race isn't worth it, and you encourage your child to disavow material possessions. Although this may be a noble gesture and sound advice, your children have the right to pursue material wealth if they so choose. They may come to the same conclusions as you; they just may need to come to them in much the same way—through experience.

It is important to empower your children to make their own decisions by letting them know that you support them in pursuing their career aspirations, however different they may be from your own. Career coaching does not mean telling them what they should do with their lives or forcing them to fit into a mold that you have created for them (however attractive that mold may seem).

This doesn't mean that you need to let them do whatever they want, without your advice and concern. Certainly you can help them think through the consequences of the options they are considering; help them consider a range of options so that they don't become locked into seeing limited possibilities for themselves. It is understandable that you want what is best for your children, that you want to save them the pain of learning the lessons you have struggled to learn. But although you can guide them, they must drive themselves: the lessons are as important as the outcome.

Do prepare yourself for possible rejection of your ideas. How will you feel if what you always wanted for your children is not what they want? How will they feel about telling you that they do not want to inherit your dreams? Be clear that each choice is one of many and that you welcome their interest or participation in your career but that you will support whatever they decide.

There is a fine line between encouragement and setting unrealistic or domineering expectations, between support and control. The bottom line is, it's their career, not yours. You are an important influence and guide, but this is not your second chance at life (Jacobsen 1998). It may be difficult to watch your child venture off into areas different from what you expected. But the alternative is that they try to please you at the expense of pleasing themselves.

THE VARTANIAN FAMILY

The Vartanian family has been in the auto leasing business since Grandfather V arrived in this country as a penniless immigrant and built a small equipment lending business into a successful and varied leasing business. Armen, the son, went happily into the business and developed it still more. Ed, the grandson, worked towards a business degree with the expectation of taking over the business himself someday. But after Ed worked in the leasing company for a few years, he began to question the assumption that he'd spend the rest of his life walking in his father's and grandfather's footsteps.

Ed finally decided that he couldn't be happy in the business and started thinking about what he really wanted to do. He felt a lot of responsibility to the family, though, and he also thought carefully about what would happen to the business without him. He discussed his dilemma with other people in the family. One young cousin, Sara, who was attending business school, told him that she'd always wanted to run a business of her own. Bingo! Ed decided to stay in the business until his cousin had her degree and was ready to take over the business. He also decided to go part-time to the Museum of Fine Arts School to pursue a life-long interest in drawing.

Several years have passed, Sara is doing very well learning the ropes, and Ed is still in the business and happy about it, now that he doesn't feel the full weight of responsibility on his shoulders. He was able to let go of the pressures upon him enough to think about what he really wanted to do in his life. For now, he's working and going to school. He thinks he might eventually combine his business skill and his artistic interest into gallery ownership or some other blended career. Now that he no longer feels responsible for the ultimate fate of the business, he's able to take the time to think about where his dreams will lead him.

From Power and Russell, *Don't Live Someone Else's Dream*, 1996

ALL IN THE FAMILY

In the 1990s television series *Mad About You*, Paul struggled with how to tell his father that he was uninterested in taking over management of the sporting goods store that had been in the family for years. The episode highlighted the need for checking assumptions. Paul had always assumed he would inherit the store, even though he was clear that it wasn't ames Champy, chairperson of CSC Index and coauthor of *Reengineering the Corporation*, learned the importance of a balanced life from a workaholic father, a general contractor who died from his third heart attack at the age of fifty-four. The elder Champy's lessons on self-reliance and independence also left his son with a reluctance to work for a large corporation, which led him to consulting.

From Lancaster, "A Father's Character, Not His Success, Shapes Kids' Careers," 1996

what he wanted to do. He dreaded the moment when he would have to say thanks but no thanks, figuring his father would be devastated. After leaving the store to his nephew, Paul's father explained to his surprised son, "I always knew this wasn't for you—you're a video director!"

It's okay and appropriate to share with your children both your career history and your own career dreams. Teach them your trade, share your knowledge, let them know that you have faith in their ability to do what you have done if that is the path they would choose. But be clear that you have no expectation that they pursue your line of work unless that's what they really want to do. Your legacy is that you have given them the strength to pursue what is important to them.

Many children will be proud and happy to take over the family tradition. One study of more than 2,000 schoolchildren suggested that more than 50 percent wanted to follow in their mother's or father's footsteps. Sometimes those interests continue, sometimes they wane over time. Sometimes the child chooses to continue what is no longer a viable vocation, such as in the case of George, who recently closed the shoe repair business that had been handed down through his family's generations. People don't repair shoes anymore, he explained to the local news media. They throw them away and buy new ones.

As your children contemplate emulating your career path, consider with them the pros and cons, the consequences and

How will your children feel about telling you that they do not want to inherit your dreams?

alternative options. Your children's choice to join your profession should be based on interest, skill, and opportunity. It is not a reflection on their respect for how you have lived your life.

THE INVOLVEMENT CONTINUUM

The degree of your involvement in your child's career decision making depends on the age of your child, the stage of career exploration he or she is in, and other specific needs and circumstances. The challenge and the ideal is to know how much involvement your child needs at any particular time and to provide it as needed. Remember your own experiences as you try to judge how much is enough and how much is too much involvement. At all times remember this is his career you are talking about, not yours. You can be involved as much as appropriate to help him make career decisions, but it is ultimately his decision to make. The guidelines provided in Exercise 1 will give you and your child a framework from which to proceed.

YOUR VARIOUS PARENTAL ROLES

In addition to how you interact with your children in the career planning process, you are an important part of all other aspects of their lives. Throughout their development, you help them understand and build relationships; you help them cope with changing physical and medical needs; and you participate with them as they explore the development of their social, political, and intellectual selves.

Therefore we do not assume that your primary role is that of career coach. Some career guidance books for parents suggest that you adopt a role identical to a professional career development specialist, but we believe that your role is much more complex, intimate, and influential. Your roles in the career planning process are interwoven with your many other parental responsibilities. You are a parent helping

EXERCISE 1

THE INVOLVEMENT CONTINUUM

Place a mark on the following continuums:

1. Amount of involvement your parents had in your career decision-making process:

   UNDERINVOLVED————————————OVERINVOLVED

   Implications/How did you react?

2. Amount of involvement you have in your children's concerns and decisions in general, not specific to career decision making (put a separate mark for each child):

   UNDERINVOLVED————————————OVERINVOLVED

   Implications/How do they react?

3. Amount of involvement you have had so far in your children's career decision making (put a separate mark for each child):

   UNDERINVOLVED————————————OVERINVOLVED

   Implications/How do they react?

4. Now ask your child(ren) to mark the last continuum to indicate the amount of involvement you are perceived as having in their career decision making. Discuss differences. Be willing to listen and to learn.

   UNDERINVOLVED————————————OVERINVOLVED

   Implications/How do they react?

EXERCISE 2

YOUR OVERALL ROLE

In your overall relationship with your children:

1. Do they generally seek your opinion and advice, or do they resist it?

2. Are you comfortable with or concerned about other aspects of their development that may help or hinder their career exploration process?

3. Are they go-getters that put ambitious energy behind everything they do, or are you generally concerned about their seeming lack of motivation?

4. What role do you play in other facets of their lives, and how do they respond to it?

with one aspect of your child's development, not a career coach who happens to be the "client's" parent. This can make career coaching roles at times easier and at times more difficult, based on your success at any given moment in other facets of your child's life. Consider the questions in Exercise 2.

The answers to these questions depend in part on your child's age, circumstances, and current challenges and in part on your success at dealing with all your parental responsibilities. As you move forward with developing your parental career coaching roles, consider the broader context in which your child is listening and responding to you.

Perhaps in an ideal world, you could say, "Now it is time to work together as career decision maker and career coach," separating the career coaching role from the role you just played when you told your children to clean up their room or when you debated curfew time or use of the family car. You could ignore your own frustration with work while you encourage your children to find a job. You could forget your own childhood and adolescent experiences and start with a clean slate.

But these parental roles are not separate from the roles you play in assisting the career planning process; rather they are an integral part of it. If your children perceive you as controlling and opinionated on other topics, there's a good chance they will also think that you are trying to dominate their career decisions. On the other hand, if your style has been laissez-faire, it will be hard for your children to believe you have a genuine interest in becoming involved with them in their career exploration. There is a fine line between being overinvolved and underinvolved. Most people fall somewhere along the continuum.

Finding the appropriate balance between giving advice and stepping aside is difficult but critical in being a help, not a hindrance, to your children's career development. They need your involvement to empower them to choose a direction that makes sense for them, based on skills, interests, values, and opportunities. This is a far more compelling and important role than molding them into what you think they should be.

Career coaching is framing the challenges of growth without robbing your child of the opportunity to develop a sense of personal authority or autonomy in decision making. Taking over that responsibility yourself can be the greatest hindrance to your child's self-respect and belief in her abilities. As Joan Didion (1961) phrased it, "Character—the willingness to accept responsibility for one's own life—is the source from which self-respect springs." That self-respect cannot grow if the child has transferred career responsibility to you or to counselors and testing processes. Your role is to offer vocabulary, questions, and frameworks to guide your children through a self-directed exploration of who they aspire to become.

EMOTIONAL INTELLIGENCE

Apprenticeship programs of the past focused on preparing young people for vocational success by providing them with technical skills and the "tools of the trade." Today employees must equip their vocational tool kits not only with technical skills and abilities but also with the ability to build rapport, show empathy, and create consensus—what psychologist Daniel Goleman (1997) defines as *emotional intelligence*. Emotional intelligence includes the ability to control one's own impulsiveness, to calm oneself, and to maintain hope in the face of setbacks.

What can parents do to begin to develop these qualities and skills in their young children? First and foremost, they must act as role models, for as Goleman points out, "having emotionally intelligent parents is itself of enormous benefit to a child." He defines the most common *inept* parenting styles as follows:

- *Ignoring feelings altogether.* Here parents will treat a child's emotional upset as a bother or as trivial, something that should be ignored. In so doing, they miss out on the opportunity to get closer to the child or to help the child learn lessons in emotional competence.

- *Being too laissez-faire.* Parents who adopt this approach will attempt to smooth all upsets, and will use bribes if necessary to get their child to stop being sad or angry, or allow inappropriate responses, such as hitting, without showing the child an alternative and more appropriate emotional response.

- *Showing no respect for how the child feels.* Parents who adopt this response pattern are typically disapproving, harsh in both their criticisms and their punishments. They will disallow any display of emotion on the child's part, and will become angry if the child tries to tell his side of the story.

All three of these styles will have long-term and detrimental effects on the child's emotional intelligence. There is, however, an effective approach to parenting in these situations, described by Goleman as the parent in the role of emotional coach or mentor. With this approach, the parent takes the child's feelings seriously enough to try to understand exactly what is upsetting him and to help him find positive ways to soothe his feelings. In order to do this, the parent must be able to distinguish his or her own, and others', emotional state (Goleman 1997). Mary Sheedy Kurcinka (2001) has written a practical guide for parents to help them help their children develop emotional intelligence. Regardless of which career path your child eventually chooses, these are qualities that are, and increasingly will be, critical to his career success. Basic skills such as the ability to work in a team, flexibility, and adaptability are found to be more important to employers than any type of specific technical work-related skills (Bynner 1997).

CLOSING COMMENTS

Remember that, like most parental actions, involvement or lack of involvement in children's decisions is usually done in good faith and with good intentions. You may have had dominating parents and swore you would back off with your own children (or vice versa). We don't question your parental judgment or sincerity; rather we offer you the opportunity to reflect on your choices and consider some options. We believe there are appropriate and inappropriate levels of parental involvement in the career decision–making process, and we offer you this book as a way to find the balance that works for you and your children. Effective career coaching can help you and your children better understand who they are and what they want from life. It can be an exciting, rewarding journey. This book provides the road map for you to use along the way.

2

LOOKING BACK AT YOUR OWN CAREER

YOU INFLUENCE YOUR CHILDREN without even trying. For the first eighteen to twenty years of their lives, they share your home and are immersed in your lifestyle. You are their first and most powerful role model. Your career satisfaction and the experience you had with your parents during your own early career exploration affect the messages you give and how you give them. Going through a process of self-examination is a first step toward enabling you to better guide your children.

THE CAREER DECISION-MAKING MODEL

Part Two of this book provides a four-step model for career decision making, as shown in Figure 1: self-assessment, identifying and exploring options, goal setting and planning, and taking action. The model is provided primarily to help you understand your role at different stages of your child's career exploration process, but a good place to begin is applying the model to your own career.

Step back and assess the direction your career is heading today and whether your current situation meets your interests, values, and skills. Use the model to reflect back on career decisions you have made throughout your lifetime. This will give you a better understanding of the career planning model that we will suggest you follow as you advise your children. Working through the questions provided in this chapter will also give you time to reflect on your own experience as a child being influenced by parental advice. You may remember early influences to your career decisions as helpful and try to emulate them, or you may want to avoid making some of the same mistakes.

FIGURE 1
*Career Decision–
Making Model*

SELF-ASSESSMENT
Interests, Values, Skills

**IDENTIFYING AND
EXPLORING OPTIONS**
*Research
Experience
Informational Interviewing*

**GOAL SETTING
AND PLANNING**
*Identifying Goals
Pinpointing Actions
Creating a Plan*

TAKING ACTION
*Job Hunting
Résumé Writing
Education*

HOW YOUR CAREER SATISFACTION AFFECTS YOUR CHILDREN

Why does your career satisfaction matter? It matters because every day you give your children messages about work through your action, your language, and your demeanor. If you consistently come home tired and grumpy after a stressful work experience, when you feel underchallenged or overchallenged by demands beyond or beneath your capabilities, then your children start to believe that making a living is a necessary evil designed to make life miserable for all those who must endure it.

On the other hand, if you come home speaking enthusiastically about a job that is important and meaningful to you, your children learn to see work as a valuable part of the human experience. You may still be tired and occasionally grumpy, but children sense the difference between happy tension and prolonged frustration. Researchers at the University of Pennsylvania and Drexel University found that parents who are happy with their jobs have the happiest and most well-adjusted children. Self-esteem as a professional seems intrinsically linked with self-esteem as a parent, and children directly benefit from it (English, 1996).

The same theory applies if you work at home. Are you satisfied or dissatisfied with your decision to do so? In this book, we define *career* as the way you lead your life. You can have a career that includes part-time work, academic work, at-home work, or nonpaid work. Our hope is that whatever you do, it is satisfying and meaningful to you. Your own behavior far outweighs what you say about career planning. The more satisfied you are about your own career, the better the chances your children will find work that is satisfying for them.

SELF-ASSESSMENT

THE MEANING OF WORK

Your children observe and learn about work through your experience and behavior. Do they learn that to have a career means giving up time with family—that is, are you a virtually absent parent because of long hours and incessant work demands? Or do they see work as one component of a balanced lifestyle? Do they learn that bosses ruin worker happiness, or that they support systems designed to help workers grow? Do they perceive that work outside the home is valued and work in the home is not? Do they develop gender stereotypes based on this perception? What do they learn about money, material possessions, and what must be done to earn them?

In the past several weeks, what have you communicated to your children about work through your experience, remarks, and behavior?

MEETING CAREER NEEDS

As you read through the remainder of these chapters, work through the steps in the career planning process for yourself before introducing them to your child. Respond to the questions in Exercises 3 and 4 to begin the career decision–making process for yourself. Career self-assessment includes analyzing your interests, values, and skills and how they are being, and can be, used and satisfied. The messages you may be unconsciously giving about work could be tied to your satisfaction or dissatisfaction in one or more of these areas. Figure 2 provides an overview of how we have defined these terms.

Interests are the things that you like to do—what fascinates, excites, and inspires you. If you are interested in what you do, you'll derive satisfaction from your work. Interests can be developed over time or tied to your personality and natural tendencies.

Values are the things that are most important to you—what motivates you and contributes to your sense of well-being. If your values are satisfied in your work, you will most likely feel committed to your job, career, and/or organization.

FIGURE 2
Defining Your Interests, Values, and Skills

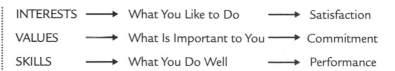

INTERESTS	→	What You Like to Do	→	Satisfaction
VALUES	→	What Is Important to You	→	Commitment
SKILLS	→	What You Do Well	→	Performance

EXERCISE 3

SELF-ASSESSMENT QUESTIONS FOR PARENTS

Before beginning the process with your children, take a minute to think through the following questions concerning your own career satisfaction and aspirations.

1. What are your interests, values, and skills?

2. How do you define success?

3. To what extent does your current situation meet these criteria?

4. When in your career history have you really been satisfied? What made that so? What made you change that situation?

5. What would you do if your career as you know it were no longer an option? What are your alternatives?

6. Where do you want to be in two, five, or ten years? What do you want to accomplish before you retire?

7. What will you do with yourself after you retire?

Skills are the things that you do well—your strengths and talents. When your skills match the requirements of your career, your performance on the job will be positively affected.

As you work with your children on their career assessment, you will be looking ahead at how they can find work that fits their interests, skills, and values. You will help them discover who they are in terms of these criteria and then help them identify work opportunities. To explore these questions for yourself, you have three frames of reference from which to look: the extent that your interests and values are being met today; what your career decisions have been throughout your lifetime; and opportunities for the future.

IDENTIFYING AND EXPLORING CAREER OPTIONS

Years ago, the career planning process was considered a one-time event. Decide as a young adult what career path to follow, gain the skills and credentials to get there, and then, as one of the pioneers of career development theory suggested, do it: find your spot and maintain it. Choice of where to enter the labor force was seen as an event in late adolescence (Herr 1997). When one of the authors of this book entered the field of career counseling, he was taught that the college-to-work transition was the fundamental and virtually irreversible first step for career development, that midcareer interventions were supplementary and were needed only for people who had character flaws that prevented them from holding a job. That is no longer true. Vocational mobility is now a necessity and is in fact a virtue. The notion of career maturity is being replaced with career adaptability: the ability to be able to change to fit new or changed circumstances (Savickas 1997).

This reality further emphasizes the need for your child—and you—to take charge of career development. Lifetime employment with one employer is no longer a viable expectation; one corporation or even one profession, such as medicine, is not going to provide all the direction and cues necessary for success.

EXERCISE 4

**IDENTIFYING
AND EXPLORING
CAREER
OPTIONS
QUESTIONS
FOR PARENTS**

1. What opportunities are currently available in your organization or career field?

2. Where can you find out more about career opportunities? What journals do you read? What was the last book you read in occupational fields that interest you? Where is your nearest source of career information or resource library?

3. Is your résumé current? When is the last time you went on an informational interview?

4. What personal development activities have you done in the past few years? What and who have been your most significant sources of learning and growth?

5. Are you satisfied that you are advancing your education in some way, either through reading, writing, direct experiences, or pursuit of a formal degree?

6. When is the last time you discussed your career with the person who pays your salary? In whom do you confide about career aspirations and struggles? Who are your present role models and mentors? What are you learning from them?

7. Name five people you would classify as most important to your career success. When is the last time you contacted them?

Our environment is dynamic and highly competitive. Without the confidence and clarity that comes from participating in career decision–making processes, you and your children could find yourselves stranded in a job and eventually downsized out of it. Consider the questions in Exercise 4.

PLANNING AND TAKING ACTION

Self-assessment and exploration are the data-gathering foundations of the career decision–making process. Unfortunately, for many people the process stops there. Career aspirations become shelved as impossible dreams. How many dying words have been laments for what could have been?

The third phase of the career decision–making process is to turn those aspirations into measurable goals, as laid out in Exercise 5, and the fourth is to take action and learn from that experience.

It takes courage to move into these stages of personal and professional growth. Dreams feel easier than possible defeat, but making a commitment to take action, even a commitment made only to oneself, is a big step forward. You may hesitate to give yourself permission to expend the energy it takes to pursue your own career satisfaction, but remember, actions speak louder than words. If your children see you setting and achieving your own career goals, taking action to be satisfied and happy with your career rather than settling for unfulfilling work and dead-end jobs, then they will more readily engage in the process of setting and striving for their own career aspirations.

As a busy parent, it may seem easier to offer advice to your children about taking action on their career plans than to take time to pay attention to your own career needs. For many people, the thought of adding one more thing to their schedule is not only frightening or anxiety producing, it seems downright impossible! That may be because they have preconceived notions of what taking action means—and their ambitious preconceptions force them into total inaction.

EXERCISE 5

GOAL-SETTING AND PLANNING QUESTIONS FOR PARENTS

Given the skills, interests, and aspirations you discovered through your own self-assessment, identify specific goals for what you want to have accomplished in:

The next year:

Three years:

Five years:

Ten years:

Before you retire:

After you retire:

TAKING SMALL STEPS TOWARD BIG GOALS

For example, say you've always wanted to practice law. You believe the only thing that would make that dream come true is to quit your job and go to law school to earn your degree. You can't afford that financially or practically at this point in your life, so you abandon the idea of practicing law altogether.

Think about other ways that you could take action toward that career goal without disrupting your entire life. Identify the skills necessary for practicing law—influencing skills, critical thinking, negotiating, listening. Identify the kinds of knowledge that you'll gather in law school—case histories, interpretation of the law, accumulation of evidence and building informed, influential arguments. Ask yourself how you could gain relevant skills and knowledge.

- Perhaps you could take on an assignment at work that requires you to do some research and build a convincing case, such as for a new project or way of accomplishing a task.

- Many workplaces offer seminars on negotiating skills, critical thinking communication skills, and problem solving. Enroll in these workshops as ways to improve your current work as well as to develop skills toward your future career.

- When you do finally relax at the end of the day, read newspapers, which are filled with present-day legal case studies. Television courtroom dramas offer you an opportunity to analyze how you might approach a case—would you do the same as the television characters or approach it differently? How do the cases you read in the newspaper compare with those on TV?

- Develop critical thinking skills by reading scholarly journals and book reviews. Play devil's advocate when reading news reports and editorials—from whose perspective are they written? What facts are being left out? How might someone else interpret the same information?

▪ Find legal information and follow conversations with attorneys on the Internet. Check out home pages of career development professionals who specialize in opportunities for people in the legal field.

None of these activities would require you to drop everything you're doing to join a degree program for aspiring attorneys, though you may identify that as a longer-term milestone toward your ultimate goal of practicing law. Be creative in thinking about your development! It's not all or nothing. Once you have identified a direction for your career, you can do little things along the way that will help you get there. The important thing is that you are moving forward and feeling positive about your ability to improve and enhance your satisfaction and employability. The more you do, the greater your confidence and competence level, and the closer you can become to doing what you really want to do with your life. Don't "foreclose" on options based on inaccurately low beliefs about your ability to be successful at them, or because of faulty understanding of what is required (Lent & Brown 1996).

COMMUNICATING YOUR CAREER ASPIRATIONS

Think about how you communicate your career goals and plans to your children. Some parents are frustrated, feeling that they have put their careers on hold in order to raise their families; they had aspirations to do great things, only to find themselves trapped in meaningless jobs for the sake of a salary. They wish they could go back to school or pursue something more meaningful but believe they must save instead for their children's future and forget their own dreams.

Without realizing it, these parents may be sending dangerous messages to their children, causing them to feel guilty about "ruining" their parents' futures and feel resented for getting in the way or confused about whether their parents really want them in their lives. Through counseling and discussion, most people with children identify parenting as one of the most important developmental activities they have ever undertaken and state that they wouldn't trade the experience for anything in the world. It is important for children to hear that, to understand that their parents can have a life outside of the role of parent and that career success and parenting can go hand in hand.

Communicate how your children's presence in your life is helping, not hindering, your personal growth. Help them understand your career goals and how they fit into them. If you are miserable at your present job, ask yourself whether you are using your parental status as an excuse to stagnate. Set goals to improve or enhance your situation, and help your children see that you are doing or aspiring to do what is right for you and for them. Sometimes it is just necessary to acknowledge the life you did not lead, and become comfortable with the decisions that you made. Otherwise, whatever you "dreamed of but never attained, lost but never mourned" will influence how you interact with your children about their careers without you realizing it (Jacobsen 1998). See Exercise 6 for further guidance.

INFLUENCES ON YOUR CAREER DECISIONS

In addition to looking at your own career in the present and future, it is important for you to look back at career decisions you have made along the way and to reflect on who influenced those decisions, as explored in Exercise 7.

People often imitate what they have themselves experienced; they manage the way they were managed and parent the way they were parented. Alternatively, if your experience with your parents regarding career growth was not positive, you may attempt to do the opposite of what was done with you. However, basing your approach to assisting your children on what worked or didn't work for you may not be the right strategy for them.

EXERCISE 6

TAKING ACTION

QUESTIONS

FOR PARENTS

1. What journals do you subscribe to that keep you up-to-date on the trends in your career field? In other career fields?

2. Do you have a career development plan? With whom do you discuss it (your manager, mentor, colleagues)? Do you find that you are able to complete your plans, or do you get frustrated that you are too busy to do the development activities that you plan?

3. What is the last professional development activity in which you participated (challenging assignment, conference, workshop, mentor relationship)?

4. In what small ways do you work toward your career goals (such as those described in question 3)? How else can you integrate developmental opportunities into your everyday activities?

5. How do you communicate with your children about your career aspirations and what you are doing to get there?

EXERCISE 7

INFLUENCES ON YOUR CAREER DECISIONS QUESTIONS FOR PARENTS

1. How did you decide which career to follow?

2. Who or what influenced your decisions?

3. What messages did your parents and other authorities give you about work?

4. What were their expectations of what you would do with your life? Did you make them proud by fulfilling those expectations, or disappoint them by following an alternative path?

5. What did your parents do for a living? How satisfied do you think they were with the way they lived their lives? Did you ever talk with them about their career satisfaction or dissatisfaction?

6. What would you have done differently, if you had known then what you know now?

YOUR PARENTS' ADVICE AND INVOLVEMENT

The final aspect of your own career to consider is how your parents influenced you, explored in Exercise 8, on page 34. Just as we have argued that your role as career coach is embedded in the larger role of parent, with its many responsibilities and complexities, so too the extent to which your career decisions were influenced by your father and mother depends on the larger context of your overall relationship with them. A good resource for thinking through your own parents' influence is *Hand Me Down Dreams* by family systems therapist and career counselor Mary Jacobsen (1999).

CLOSING COMMENTS

In this chapter, we have encouraged you to consider your current level of career satisfaction and the influences on your early career decisions. You have looked from a broad perspective at your general relationships with your children and with your own parents. We encourage you to read the rest of the book with this broad context in mind.

EXERCISE 8

PARENTAL INFLUENCE QUESTIONS FOR PARENTS

Think back to your relationship with your parents as you grew up and into adulthood.

1. Did you seek their advice or rebel against it?

2. In what ways do your children's reactions to your suggestions remind you of how you reacted to suggestions made by your parents?

3. Were your parents forceful in their opinions and expect you to follow their every word, or did they encourage you to form your own position?

4. Did your mother and your father have different expectations of you?

5. How did you react to their parenting styles? To what extent does your parenting style mirror or reject the styles of those who parented you?

3

LOOKING FORWARD TO YOUR CHILD'S CAREER

The single best predictor of success is the ability to learn from experience. Our experiences shape how we view and operate in the world. The paradox parents face is that the world is constantly changing, which in some ways dilutes the value of career planning. Looking back on your own career helps you understand your perspectives on work and how you are approaching the career coaching process with your children. But to help them move forward with their own careers, you may sometimes need to abandon long-held beliefs that no longer match the requirements of your children's workplace.

For example, many of us grew up in academic and professional environments where individual achievement was expected and rewarded. We would strive to be the best and

CHART 3	From	To
	Employment security	Employability
	Loyalty to one company	Focus on profession
	Having a job	Doing important work
THE NEW EMPLOYMENT CONTRACT	Company taking care of employees	Company empowering employees
	Employment for life	Mutual benefit employment

often did so with little help. Instilling an ethic of excellence and achievement will help your child in the twenty-first-century work environment. The emphasis will continue to shift, however, from individual accomplishment to cross-functional team collaboration. Employees will be evaluated as team members. It's no longer considered cheating to collaborate; it is expected.

THE "NEW" EMPLOYMENT CONTRACT

In the past, there was an unwritten contract: The workplace offered job security in exchange for good, hard work. Companies took care of employees' careers and provided a stepwise progression "up the ladder" based on seniority and performance. Companies had dependable, loyal employees, and employees had job security, a good salary, and fringe benefits (DeMeuse & Tornow, 1993).

The "new contract," as outlined in Chart 3, still unwritten but increasingly understood, shows some major shifts that call into question the traditional linear views of career progress (Herr 1997). "Work relationships are now based on short-term mutual investments of added value: workers contribute their skills, knowledge, time, energy and creativity to create tangible results. In return, employers offer workers financial compensation, training and development, work experience, a chance to prove their abilities, and opportunities to build valuable relationships with people who may be able to help them in the future" (Tulgan 1999). Both parties understand that job security cannot be guaranteed and the bond between them has changed (DeMeuse & Tornow 1993).

This new employment contract is not necessarily bad news for employees. Mutual benefit employment goes both ways: employees stay at a company for as long as the company needs their talents and skills or for as long as the company is providing them with the best professional opportunity. Corporations now struggle to find and retain the skilled employees needed to meet their business objectives. The more you have to offer the workplace, the greater the demands for your skills. Your ability to add value is what makes all the difference (Tulgan 1999).

Career decision making, once viewed as a single stage of growth in the college years, is now a lifetime skill. The changing employment contract not only affects your child's need for ongoing professional development and career mobility; it also requires you to participate in the same kind of ongoing self-assessment. In our parents' and grandparents' generations, it was not unusual for people to stay with one employer for the duration of their careers. They used their own stability as a model of what we were to emulate. But the workplace has changed, and that model no longer applies. You as a worker—let alone you as a parent—need to constantly engage in a process of career renewal. A periodic examination of your own skills and career options, like the one in Exercise 9, will help to ensure your satisfaction and your readiness to move on as job changes and circumstances demand.

Understanding the new contract is important as you explore your options and research how you might enhance your present job or prepare to move on. It may be of less concern for your children, who will grow up in an era when expectations for lifetime employment are not as prevalent as they were when you or your parents joined the workforce. We put "new contract" in quotations because though this trend is new for many parents and people from the baby

EXERCISE 9

YOUR EXPERIENCE WITH THE NEW EMPLOYMENT CONTRACT QUESTIONS FOR PARENTS

1. Have you ever lost your job due to a restructuring or downsizing? How did you react? Did your career path shift toward new directons because of it? Do you feel better or worse off because of those shifts?

2. Do you participate in ongoing professional development activities? What else do you do to make yourself more and more employable and in demand?

3. What kinds of unwritten contracts do you believe operated in your parents' day compared to now? How might the workplace operate when your children are your age?

boom generation, it is the only work paradigm known by most people entering the labor force today. As Bruce Tulgan (1998) found out when interviewing hundreds of people in their twenties, "Most of us (Generation X) would never dream of building a career around a long-term affiliation with one established company. Those of our generation have always known that the only success and security we will ever have is that which we build from within ourselves."

Be careful about painting visions of gloom about the options for your children's future, especially if you yourself face a layoff or job uncertainty. Refrain from statements such as, "It used to be that companies took care of their people; today they just care about profits." Help your children understand the importance of continuously upgrading their skills and developing confidence in their abilities, and to see each job as a learning opportunity. Instead of lamenting the fact that your current job has ended, celebrate how much more qualified you are now as a result of having that work experience. Your reactions to the realities of the new workplace will inform and influence your children, especially younger ones.

WORK AS SOURCE OF IDENTITY

The process of developing a vocational identity is integral to the process of overall identity development (Blustein, Devenis, & Kidney 1989; Vondracek 1993). In the past, people identified themselves as an employee of a company, and took pride in their years of tenure and the comfort and rewards they brought. One of our career counseling clients shared the difficulty of being laid off after eleven years and coping with the idea of not having a business card. His identity was tied to being an employee of the company, and it was difficult for him to give up having the small piece of paper that defined who he was.

The realities of the new workforce bring support for the theory of the "life-space" approach to career planning (Super 1984; Savickas 1997). Work is an important part of a person's life, but it is not the only role people play. Work roles must be viewed in context with other life roles, such as spouse, parent, friend, and spiritual human being. With the rising use of contingency and temporary workforces (Robinson 2003; Reich 2001; Herr 1997), people must find their sense of identity from within their professional achievements, not from a particular company or organization.

WORKPLACE TRENDS

Like the changes illustrated in our discussion of the new employment contract, other trends exist for which your child

BABETTE'S STORY

Consider the example of Babette, a lively and outgoing person who as a small child rushed to the center of every party where she would dance and entertain. She was a natural noisemaker, with the potential to become a performer, a salesperson, or perhaps a teacher. Unfortunately, her parents were embarrassed by what they saw as a clamoring for attention and stifled the growth of her natural kinesthetic aptitude for performance and human interaction.

Her father was a successful chemical engineer who thought that the future would be bright for a woman entering the field that he had enjoyed. He cared about Babette and worked with her on homework each night. He selected her courses so that she would have a proper foundation for the chemical engineering curriculum that would eventually lead her to one lonely research job after another. The fact that science came hard for her kept her from extracurricular activities such as the school's theater and student government in which she longed to participate. She was allowed to attend dancing class on Saturdays until the money for that class was diverted into a special tutoring program to help boost her science scores on the SAT.

Babette entered therapy in her mid-thirties after a breakdown, which her therapist blamed on long periods of enforced isolation. She was earning $60,000 a year as a chemical engineer but she was desperately unhappy. She had never had a chance to develop her personal self-esteem because almost every aspect of her life was guided and decided by her parents. A critical factor in Babette's story was her failure to develop "personal authority," or responsibility for her own decisions. Another critical factor was the mismatch between her natural abilities and aspirations and the career path she followed on the advice of her well-intentioned parents. They were not cruel; they helped her enter a field where there were opportunities and the potential for good income. When she had her breakdown, her parents were shocked. They had supported her in every way, she had a good job and a good income—what else was there that she could want?

must be prepared, as listed in Chart 4. The world of work is indeed changing. Sharing your own stories and experiences is an important component of your career coaching role, but you cannot rely on the past to help prepare your children for the future.

Given these general trends, to be most helpful in discussing career opportunities and requirements with your children,

CHART 4 **SOME** **WORKPLACE** **TRENDS**	■ Individual achievement is being replaced by team focus. Strong interpersonal skills will become a condition of employment. ■ Large corporations are becoming leaner and flatter. There is an increase in employment in small companies. Career paths are changing. Downsizing is a way of life. Outplacement is a real possibility. The use of contingency and temporary work-forces, and employee leasing, is increasing. ■ Continuous lifelong learning will be essential. Companies will provide professional development opportunities and learning assignments in place of job security.

■ The focus will be on psychological success versus upward mobility. There are few one-job, one-employer careers. Employees are increasingly expected to manage their own careers.

■ Employees must know and be able to communicate their skills, values, interests, etc. People who take risks and think creatively will be valued and rewarded.

■ We are moving toward a more diverse workforce. New hires are entering a global economy.

■ The "virtual workplace" offers increased opportunities for telework, long-distance communications, and a focus on results.

■ To stay competitive, organizations will continuously re-create themselves. These "self-designing" organizations require employees who can continuously adapt and grow. No organization is exempt.

■ The world is becoming increasingly technology and computer dependent. Fifty-five percent of U.S. corporation capital investments are related to information technology. Technological improvements will replace unskilled labor.

■ Relative wages are declining. Wage gaps will grow larger between occupational and educational levels. Highly skilled workers will be required in all industries.

Adapted from Montross and Shinkman, "Which Work Are We Preparing Students For?," 1996

It is necessary to pay attention to job availability and workforce trends, but it is not possible to learn them all. The focus should be on assessing major areas of interest and then looking at corresponding trends.

- Understand what these trends mean and help your children think about how to be prepared for them.

- Talk with your own employer and colleagues to stay current on workforce trends and professional skills requirements in your occupational field. Share these learnings with your children.

- Learn together about specific trends in their areas of interest by attending seminars, browsing in bookstores, and speaking with experts.

- Expose your children to multiple opportunities for developing skills that they will need in the future—regardless of the specific work they choose to do. For example, help them identify teams to work and play on and discuss how to work most effectively as a team member.

- Encourage them to socialize with a diverse group of friends and to be open to multiple perspectives and ways of doing things. Expose them to diverse cultures and ways of living. Encourage—don't avoid—discussions about how people are different from each other.

- Provide opportunities for your children to develop technological skills such as computer literacy, and instill a love of learning and discovery at an early age. This doesn't require huge investments in computer equipment (though consider educational software rather than video games when selecting gifts).

- Visit your local library often; find out if the school computer lab can be used after hours; help your children identify volunteer opportunities that may expose them to computer technology. If you know nothing about computers, learn together! Otherwise, share what you know.

These trends and suggestions go beyond helping your children with their careers. They will help develop skills needed for success not just at work but in life overall. Like helping them develop emotional intelligence, helping your children work as team players and excel as part of a diverse learning society is part of your role as parental coach that transcends but is integral to the career decision–making process.

OCCUPATIONAL TRENDS

Two articles (Milmore 1996; Eng 1996) express similar worries that parents are often out of step with today's emerging job markets. "Career service professionals warn that inaccurate or outdated information, coupled with a parent's own emotions, can pressure young graduates to turn away from low-paying or nonprofit opportunities, head into what parents consider the 'hottest' fields, or take a job only to realize a parent's own unfulfilled dream" (Eng 1996).

Nevertheless, parents cannot become experts at all the occupational trends—they change too fast and there are too many of them! "When the first census was taken more than 200 years ago, workers were classified into just three occupational categories. Today, there are more than 30,000 occupations to choose from" (Otto 1996). Parents will naturally know more about some fields and less about others. Keeping up with occupational and market trends is a full-time job.

However, you and your child need to learn how to access information quickly in areas that are identified through your child's skills and interest assessment process. Luckily, there are many excellent resources available dedicated to the task of providing up-to-date information on job growth and decline, salary information, and job requirements. Because the information is readily available elsewhere, and because it becomes outdated quickly, we have chosen to include a comprehensive guide to accessing the information in the Parent Tool Kit section rather than duplicating efforts by listing current occupational outlooks here. We strongly urge you to familiarize yourself and your child with the resources available through your local library and career center and online via the Internet. Quarterly updates are available through the Department of Labor Statistics (in a periodical called the *Occupational Outlook Quarterly*), and most major newspapers carry summaries of the trends as soon as they are released.

It is necessary to pay attention to job availability and work-force trends, but it is not necessary or possible to learn them all. The focus should be on assessing major areas of interest first and then narrowing them down by looking at corresponding trends. Fortunately, there are many online and print resources available to help you and your child search for specific fields and trends. Learning that process of research is as important as learning a specific skill.

PART TWO

COACHING YOUR CHILD

THROUGH CAREER DISCOVERY

N PART ONE, we defined career coaching and talked about some of the benefits of taking on that responsibility. We also asked you to think about your own career and assess your current career status by going through a four-step process and by reflecting back on the influence and involvement of your parents in your decisions. Finally, we described the world of work your child will face, a place quite different from that in which your career developed. In Part Two, we focus in depth on the four steps in career decision making that we recommend any decision maker follow, and then we define a corresponding role that you can play as your child works her way through them. Keep in mind that children differ in their readiness to begin the process in earnest and in the ease with which they are able to move through it.

The key for you as parent is to try to understand where your child is in the process and to play the role that is appropriate. As stated earlier, the process is not necessarily a linear one. Your child may cycle back through earlier steps as she gains greater clarity or explores and then abandons career options that at an earlier stage seemed like a perfect fit. In broad terms, the four steps in the career decision–making model and their corresponding career coaching roles are shown in Chart 5, on pages 48–49.

When your child first starts to think seriously about careers, you should encourage her to spend time on self-assessment, the process of careful and thorough gathering of data about herself with specific regard to skills, interests, abilities, and personality. In Part Three, we provide you with a listing of resources that you can use in your role as Clarifier, which is the role of helping your child clarify and make meaning out of the data generated during this assessment phase. An in-depth discussion of your role at this stage is presented in Chapter 4. This is perhaps the most difficult role for you to play, and the most important as well, for it is our collective experience that many people want to skip over this important first step and proceed directly to steps 2, 3, or 4. It is, however, the most critical step, for doing it well results in greater likelihood of finding a good fit and therefore in career satisfaction and success. Again, remember that your child has to make meaning of the data for herself, and you, in the role of Clarifier, can play a vital part.

Having devoted time to that assessment, your child, with your help as Connector, moves into the second stage of the process, that of identifying and exploring options. The role of Connector has at least two meanings here. First, it means helping your child link or connect the data gathered in self-assessment to career options consistent with the data. Will the options so identified provide satisfaction because they are of interest to him? Are they likely to lead to real commitment to the work because the work is believed to be important and consistent with his values? Will his performance be maximized because he is using his natural skills and talents to the fullest? Will the work be appropriate for someone with his personality characteristics? These are the types of questions you as Connector might help your son answer. A second meaning of the term *Connector* as we define it here is someone who can help by connecting up your child with the appropriate resources to do a thorough job of exploring several career options, thus encouraging the process of looking before leaping.

Your child is now ready for some narrowing of choices, for setting of goals, for creating a plan of action. As she moves into this third phase of career decision making, you will shift to the role of Challenger, helping her set goals that will stretch her but that are attainable and appropriate. How often have we seen talented young people falter at this point and set goals for themselves that clearly will not lead to a satisfying career choice? As Challenger, you can assist in this important phase, but be aware that you and your child may also need to revisit the earlier steps of self-assessment and option identification.

Finally your child is ready to implement the plan, whether that means selecting a college or graduate program or conducting a job search. Armed with the knowledge gathered in the first three steps, the child approaches this action stage in control and confident in a chosen path. Your role here is that of Motivator, keeping the momentum going, checking progress, motivating when he or she falters and flounders. In Chapter 7, you will find detailed suggestions and resources for this, the last of your four roles.

Because of the changing nature of the world of work as described in Chapter 3, you may be expected to call upon these four roles on several occasions over the course of your child's career. Once learned, however, we believe they provide you with a specific set of interrelated coaching skills that will prove invaluable to your child as he or she encounters the ever-changing future.

CHART 5

FOUR COACHING ROLES

If your child...	He/she needs...	You can help your child by...	Specific things you can do include...
• Is unsure of future plans • Has not yet given serious thought to careers • Has too many options under consideration	Help with self-assessment of interests, skills, values, and natural strengths and talents	Helping CLARIFY what he or she might want to do and would be good at	• Support natural interests and abilities • Ask questions to help narrow and expand their thinking • Provide a variety of experiences • Partner with guidance counselors and support in-school career activities

STEP 1: SELF-ASSESSMENT   YOUR ROLE = CLARIFIER

If your child...	He/she needs...	You can help your child by...	Specific things you can do include...
• Is clear about interests but not how to apply them • Has identified a few options he or she is interested in pursuing	To research and get experience and first-hand information about these *options*	CONNECTING him or her to people, resources, and potential work experiences	• Help connect self-assessment with options and possibilities • Suggest relevant reading (subscriptions, books, articles) • Introduce him or her to your network • Encourage gaining experience and a broadened perspective

STEP 2: IDENTIFYING AND EXPLORING OPTIONS   YOUR ROLE = CONNECTOR

CHART 5 CONT.

FOUR COACHING ROLES

If your child...	He/she needs...	You can help your child by...	Specific things you can do include...
STEP 3: GOAL SETTING AND PLANNING		**YOUR ROLE = CHALLENGER**	
▪ Is creating plans and establishing goals for the future ▪ Has reached a milestone and needs help with next steps	To understand the importance and characteristics of good *goals*, including a backup plan	**CHALLENGING** him or her to set appropriate goals	▪ Help connect self-assessment and options to specific milestones and goals ▪ Consider workplace trends and viability of goals ▪ Help set realistic but flexible goals
STEP 4: TAKING ACTION		**YOUR ROLE = MOTIVATOR**	
▪ Is getting ready for initial job or academic program ▪ Is preparing to move on to another opportunity	▪ Help with job hunting, résumé writing, and interview skills ▪ Information about opportunities	**MOTIVATING** him or her to take action	▪ Explore educational and/or job options ▪ Visit colleges or vocational schools ▪ Review and critique résumé ▪ Conduct practice interviews ▪ Identify mentors

SELF-ASSESSMENT

PARENT AS CLARIFIER

NOW THYSELF" is an ancient motto of success. Self-assessment, the deliberate increase in self-understanding, is the starting place of the four-step cycle of career decision making. From the beginning, it is important for the parent to teach this process as a lifetime skill. Career decision making is no longer a linear event ending in attainment of a single goal—getting a particular job, entering college or graduate school, or getting into one of the armed services.

Similarly, the career decision–making process is not linear or strictly sequential—it is a feedback system. Careers do not follow static polarized definitions: they are dynamic human events, and for most people there are multiple career alternatives. A person must make choices and set priorities based on an assessment of skills, interests, values, capabilities, and opportunities.

The process happens over and over again in a lifetime. In the same way that sports teams have different strategies in different periods of the game, your child will have one set of strategies in the establishment phase of her career, as she learns to maintain her early success, and another set in late career when age discrimination and other factors are in play. What in the past were considered static careers—medicine, law, academia—are now as fluid as careers in entertainment, sales, and marketing. Medical doctors face enormously important career decisions well into their establishment as practitioners. Those persons who choose medicine to gain some stability and freedom from career dynamics are surprised and often disappointed when they learn that their field has also become subject to universal forces of vocational change. In fact, the forces of change have displaced the forces of continuity in every career field.

> *Careers do not follow static, polarized definitions: they are dynamic human events, and for most people there are multiple career alternatives.*

AREAS FOR ASSESSMENT

In the self-assessment phase of the career decision–making process, there are five distinct areas of human experience that need evaluation, clarification, and growth:

- Interests
- Skills
- Values
- Personality
- Emotional intelligence

In thinking about each of these five areas of assessment, it is useful to reflect on something Ralph Waldo Emerson wrote in his essay on self-reliance:

The objection to conforming to usages that have become dead to you, is that it scatters your force. It loses your time and blurs the impression of your character. . . . Do your thing, and I shall know you. Do your work, and you shall reinforce yourself. Insist on yourself; never imitate. Your own gift you can present every moment with the cumulative force of a whole life's cultivation; but of the adopted talent of another you have only an extemporaneous half possession. That which each can do best, none but his Maker can teach him. No man yet knows what it is, nor can, till that person has exhibited it.

Assessment is the search for that which needs to be exhibited in our career if we are to be happy and successful.

ASSESSING CAREER INTERESTS— SOURCES OF CAREER SATISFACTION

In a competitive world, vocational happiness often gets short shrift. Many parents and career advisors find themselves saying, "To find your work interesting is simply asking too much. At best, work is just a source of income. Look for satisfaction in your family and hobbies and community service. To ask for more is not being realistic. If you don't make a major splash by the time you're thirty, it's over."

However, a somewhat contradictory notion keeps popping up in the literature of career development: Following your own vocational interest pattern is a key variable in success. In other words, to be successful, your child needs to be doing work for which she has some affinity. Long-term career satisfaction is vital to long-term success, because to sustain success we need to be fascinated, excited, inspired, interested in our work.

To bring order out of the chaos of our possibilities, we must impose focus, goals, intentions—that is, we need self-control. The reality that emerges from possibility grows in some degree from our capacity for such self-control. Children begin the journey of learning first by learning to concentrate, to control the content of the mind—not allowing it to be overrun with worry, sexual preoccupations, or whatever is nonproductive. If your child does not learn how to focus his thoughts, his mind will direct itself unconsciously, zeroing in on the most attractive problem of the moment rather than on the most important problem.

DEFINING INTERESTS

The word *interest* comes from the root *inter*—"to be between." Interests reflect the event that takes place between the subject and the object. Career interests are the concerns, curiosity, or simple attention that occurs between a personality and a career. Interests in careers, like interests in books, or colors, or sports, will vary from individual to individual. The sources of interests are rooted in genetic dispositions and in learned or acquired behaviors conditioned by opportunity. A child may have a natural interest in sailing but never have the opportunity to develop that interest because of socioeconomic limitations. Another child, who watches popular cartoon shows, may want to become a Power Ranger only to be shocked to learn that that career does not exist in reality.

Nature and nurture usually combine in some way to give us a profile of career interests. One of the best standardized measures of such interest patterns is the *Strong Interest Inventory®*, instrument, available in most high schools and colleges or from one of the career counseling resources you can read about in the Parent Tool Kit section. To learn more about how interests work to shape careers, look at *Real People, Real Jobs* (Montross et al., 1995), which introduces you to forty individuals in a variety of work environments, all of whom struggled to establish congruency between themselves and their work.

CLASSIFYING INTERESTS

One of the great strides in deciphering career development patterns was the classification of careers based on interests. Persons with certain broad patterns of interests are attracted to certain career areas; thus interests are in a very real way the core building blocks of a satisfying career.

Through standardized tools such as the *Strong,* parents can help children understand the significance of interests. It is an important step forward when the parent affirms that the child's interests are credible and relevant to the career decision–making process. Parental desire to understand what interests the child gives that child a feeling of authenticity and personal power. A tool such as the *Strong* can then help the child to chart her interests and see how those interests relate to people in real jobs.

One of the great values of the *Strong* is in helping your child understand his underlying career motivators—his general occupational orientation. The General Occupational Themes in the *Strong* draw upon the work of John Holland (1985), who found that in American society most people identify with one or more of six types and each person may be characterized using the descriptors of one type or some combination of these types as listed in Chart 6.

Beyond describing individuals, Holland found that occupational environments can also be described by one of six types and each environment attracts a particular type of person. Thus the personal types of co-workers, as much as job requirements, establish the psychosocial culture of a given organization. Supporting data in unpublished studies of hiring criteria done by outplacement firms consistently rank attitude, business philosophy, and comfort level (Do you fit in? Do I, the employer, want to spend eight to ten hours a day with you over the next five years?) ahead of experience, knowledge, and skills as important factors in the selection process.

CHART 6		People	Work Environments
PEOPLE AND THEIR WORK ENVIRONMENTS BY HOLLAND THEME	Realistic	Strong mechanical, psychomotor, and athletic abilities; honest; loyal; like the outdoors; prefer working with machines, tools, plants, and animals	Structured; clear goals and lines of authority; work with hands, machines, or tools; casual dress; focus on tangible results; engineering, military, skilled trades
	Investigative	Strong problem solving and analytical skills; mathematically inclined; like to observe, learn, and evaluate; prefer working alone; reserved; idea generators	Nonstructured; research oriented; intellectual; discover, collect, and analyze ideas/data; science, math, medicine, and computer related; labs, universities, high tech, hospitals
	Artistic	Creative; complex; emotional; intuitive; idealistic; flair for communicating ideas; prefer working independently; like to sing, write, act, paint, think creatively	Nonstructured; creative; flexible; rewards unconventional and aesthetic values; creation of products and ideas; arts organizations, film/TV, publishing, advertising, museums, theater, galleries
	Social	Friendly, outgoing; find fulfillment in helping others; strong verbal and personal skills, teaching abilities, impulsive	Harmonious; congenial; work on people-related problems/issues; inform, train, develop, cure, or enlighten others; team oriented; human resources; training, education, social service, hospitality, health care, nonprofit
	Enterprising	Confident; assertive; sociable; speaking and leadership abilities; like to use influence; strong interpersonal skills, status conscious	True business environment; results oriented; driven; high-quality service and product orientation; entrepreneurial; high prestige; power focused; sales, management, politics, finance, retail, leadership
	Conventional	Dependable; disciplined; precise; persistent; orderly; efficient; practical; detail oriented; clerical and numerical abilities	Ordered; clear rules and policies; systematized manipulation and organization of data; control and handling of money; high income potential; accounting, business, finance, administration

Holland found in his research that we enjoy congenial environments in which we can exercise our skills and abilities, express our attitudes and values, solve interesting problems, and generally find roles that are stimulating and satisfying. A congenial environment also allows us to engage in interesting tasks or responsibilities while generally avoiding those we find distasteful or uninteresting. Our career decision making takes place at the intersection of our personality and the personality of our work environment. Success, satisfaction, and stability all rely on our choice of environments that fit our personality. Most people and most specific work roles have descriptors that are a combination of two or three themes. Using all possible combinations of all six types creates more than 720 possible classifications.

Discrepancies between your self-perceived Theme preferences and your actual living/working environment cause vocational dissatisfaction even when the job you have is satisfying in some ways. In such cases, your work is often blamed for your lack of recreation and vocational satisfaction. For instance, an Enterprising-Realistic woman may fulfill the Enterprising part of her personality by working in real estate sales and the Realistic side by leisure activities that require mechanical skills and ingenuity to produce tangible products. If for some reason she is expected to attend theater performances and art exhibits at the expense of her Realistic interests, she may find herself bored and feeling obligated rather than entertained. The misery quotient is clearly traced to her avocational activity, but the dissatisfaction expresses itself quite often as dissatisfaction with her work: "I am too busy!" In reality, she is not choosing what is good for her.

The *Strong Interest Inventory* and Holland *Self-Directed Search* assessments are available in most high schools and colleges or from one of the career counseling resources listed in the Parent Tool Kit section of this book.

LETTING NATURAL INTERESTS EMERGE

Parents need to watch for natural interests and support their development. Providing an environment rich in opportunities to express interests and preferences is perhaps the single most valuable gift any parent can bestow on a child. Interest patterns emerge from the expression and experience of preferences among options. Having options is critical to growth, and learning how to create options for oneself is an important success skill. If we never have the opportunity to express or experience a preference, we do not understand that it is real.

The philosophical question about whether a tree falling in the woods makes a sound if no one is there to hear it is in a sense similar to the problem of unexhibited interests: Do they exist? The experience of many career counselors is that unexpressed interests do exist and can cause trauma if left repressed. One of the signs of depression is lethargy and disinterest in the environment. Vocational depression is similar: nothing appeals; nothing looks interesting. Vocational de-pression at midlife is not typical in the general population; however, it is not unusual in someone experiencing career distress.

Parents, teachers, and professional helpers are sources of data and information, but, as Shakespeare said, "To thine own self be true."

Theme preferences help your child understand the following:

- What kinds of jobs and occupations she might like

- What activities he values

- The type of work environments in which she is comfortable

- Colleagues he wants to be around

- The sorts of problems she likes to tackle

Theme preferences on the *Strong* give your child a good measure of the diversity in her interests and ask her to think about how that diversity finds expression in her daily life and work. Themes with low preferences may be telling her about arcas she might want to avoid or in which she has little concrete experience.

In the story of Babette described earlier, Babette was never given a sense that her interests were important or even reliable data that should be taken into account. The critical factor in self-assessment is the individual's complete participation, at any age. Parents, teachers, and professional helpers are sources of data and information, but, as Shakespeare said, "To thine own self be true." No one but you can or should tell you how to choose your career.

ASSESSING CAREER SKILLS— SOURCES OF SUCCESSFUL PERFORMANCE

"Do what you do best." That adage is at the core of most career self-help literature. Discovering career skills is largely a function of education and opportunity. To paraphrase Ralph Waldo Emerson, we don't know what we can do until we do it.

REDEFINING JOB SECURITY

In the twenty-first century, our skills will always be changing in response to changing technology. However, we need to focus on what comes naturally. Nothing is easy, but some skills will seem more natural to your child in the way that writing is more natural with one hand than the other. Furthermore, if you force a left-handed child to write with the right hand, all kinds of psychological problems will emerge.

The twentieth-century career structure emphasized commitment to one career for life, based on nineteenth-century values such as routine production, economies of scale, and structural stability. The economy in which most of us matured stressed job security and favored a static long-term loyalty to the employer; the conventional wisdom dictated finding your one right career track and passively staying in place, more or less dependent on your employer for opportunities and growth. Job security meant a kind codependency.

That world is largely gone but not forgotten. In the twenty-first-century work environment, job security is a thing of the past. What in the twentieth century was called *job security* has evolved into something called *employability*. Our sense of security in this new age will be found in our toolbox of skills and experiences, in our attitude toward work, in what we contribute, in what we do that is fantastic, in what we do that makes us employable—not in passive dependency on our employer or on a set of unchanging skills. Our children need to hear the message that skills assessment is a lifetime process: new tasks, new assignments, new opportunities give us a chance to try our hand at new skills.

ASSESSING SKILLS AND TALENTS

One of the difficult lessons in assessment of skills is helping the child to learn the difference between easy and natural. Nothing is easy; even natural skills require work. The most gifted prodigy goes nowhere without patience, practice, and perseverance.

Some skills can be assessed by aptitude surveys, although the most reliable source of data on skills is incremental experience. As we will find in Chapter 6, the parent as Challenger is an important role in the career planning process. However, that role plays out here in the skills assessment process as well. Parental support is vital in the period when self-doubts set in: the child needs support to keep on, to resist the temptation to quit too soon. Parental support is also vital in cases where tutors and trainers are providing negative feedback but the child has developed commitment and a faith in her eventual ability to succeed.

Skills drive performance, but talent is always second to motivation in determining success. Children are often so aptitude conscious that talent seems more important to them than desire and persistence. Therefore, when parents talk with children about skills and talent, it is crucial to explain the importance of attitude.

Furthermore, although most career skills are not dependent on hand-eye coordination or artistic or musical ability, athletics, drawing, and singing are a common core of early curricula, making children believe that all skills are similar to these specific skills. Children often think you either can hit a ball or you can't; you either can draw a horse or you can't; you either can sing a song or you can't. They are very sensitive to these thresholds of natural ability. But they must come to understand that most success is the product of a modicum of skill and a mountain of motivation.

Another area of concern in skills assessment is differentiating between skills you want for your own enjoyment and skills you need to earn a living. Parents must let children know that many gifted artists cannot make a living by selling their work, but parents also have a significant role in legitimizing the development of natural skills that may or may not have commercial potential.

Perhaps the most important new concept in the area of skills development is that of multiple intelligences. Psychologists and educators are now stressing the importance of looking for seeds of intelligence in a whole variety of areas within the span of human ability: kinesthetic, spatial, musical, linguistic, logical, quantitative, interpersonal, persuasive, influential. A person can be bright and gifted and affirmed in all kinds of ways.

ASSESSING CAREER VALUES—SOURCES OF MEANING

Meaningful work has become a Holy Grail, something one strives for but never grasps. The reality is that meaning and a sense of value are critical to sustained career satisfaction. The word *meaning* grew out of words for *purpose* and *intention*. Values give us purpose. We cannot define goals

REMEMBERING ALL THE ROADS NOT TAKEN

Once upon a time, Marsha Shapiro of Manhattan took a test called the *Strong Interest Inventory*. It doesn't identify specific talents, but it asks people how they enjoy spending their time and correlates the responses to those given by people in specific occupations.

Ms. Shapiro's scores were highest in the "creative, like to work alone" category. She became an account executive and writer at a government agency. "As a writer, I did enjoy working alone," she says. "But that didn't stop me when, about two years ago, an opportunity came my way."

The position of director of advertising and promotion opened up in her department, and her boss urged her to apply. "My ego and my wallet," she says, "drove me to act on his suggestion."

"So," she writes, "I landed the job and left my solitary cubicle for the maelstrom of a director's office, where a staff of account executives and writers began reporting to me."

It wasn't long before the recognition and congratulations faded, and Ms. Shapiro found herself attending meetings, completing reports, directing staff, and resolving conflicts. She was spending very little time working alone and no time on hands-on creative work. "It was getting hard to deny that I was unhappy,"

she writes. "Work wasn't fun anymore."

Finally she went to her boss and told him she wasn't happy, that she missed creative work. "He tried to talk me out of it, told me I was doing a great job, that I was making a mistake," she says.

After a time, she resumed her work as a writer. "How do I feel about it now?" she says. "Well, the boss who promoted me left over a year ago. I don't know whether my new boss knows this story, but she likes my writing. I sometimes think about the perks and the money and what might have been but know they aren't what make me glad to come to work every day."

New York Times, January 7, 1996

and direction apart from our career values. Children have values, and parents can help children authenticate those values; they can help children verify that values exist and understand the part values play in decision making. Whenever a child says, "This is important to me—this is something I care about," the child is staking out a value. We as parents need to celebrate that moment of growth. For example, if an early value is justice for animals, that value may shape a career as a veterinarian or an ecologist.

DEFINING CAREER VALUES

The word *value* comes from words denoting "to be worth something." Unlike interests and skills, which have greater tangibility, values describe the process of assigning worth and significance to dimensions of a career, or a job, or a life. Career values help us assign relative merit and importance to aspects of our work. Concern about values seems to be at an all-time high; by our count, 25 percent of the books on the *New York Times* best-seller list are about values and meaning and the metaphors by which we experience transpersonal reality.

Our values tell us what is important to us. Values shape our pride, our commitments, our integrity, the kind of future we are trying to bring about. David Hume observed in 1748 that ambition, avarice, self-love, vanity, friendship, generosity, and public spirit, mixed in various degrees and distributed through society, have been, from the beginning of the world, the source of all the actions and enterprises ever observed among humankind. Our children can build a future based on compassion and generosity if we support them in their day-to-day efforts to be compassionate and generous.

CLASSIFYING VALUES

The dominant career values in the United States are *economic*. We tend to value our work and our contribution by the size of our paycheck. There is a sense of free market competition in all the economic values. If our primary or core values are economic, then we come to value those interests and skills for which we are compensated. In a market economy, we all are selling something. What others will buy from us can shape our valuing of skills and competence. Thus, whereas commonplace guidance in the 1950s was "learn how to type," the commonplace guidance of the twenty-first century will probably be "learn how to sell." Other economic values arising in the marketplace are accountability, honesty, fairness, promise keeping, excellence, and integrity.

A second values cluster that ranks high in the United States is what we might call *love*. This includes valuing work that does no harm, work that helps, cares for, empowers. Altruism, fidelity, social service, empathy, sympathy, caring, respect, and compassion all are encompassed by this second values grouping.

A third prominent values cluster is *leadership*. These are values related to the accumulation and exercise of power, control, political influence, and dominance. A related cluster of values, but one that some career counselors consider to have its own identity, can be called *adventure*. This includes the values related to overcoming adversity, taking risks, being independent, going where there is no path.

Other values clusters include *aesthetic*, valuing the experience of beauty, grace, form, creativity, intuition, freedom from convention; *theoretical*, valuing the quest for knowledge, bringing order out of chaos, systematizing of information and facts or things; *spiritual*, valuing the unifying encounter with the cosmos and with the Other, expressing an inner wholeness, seeking knowledge of transcendent reality either through a religious tradition or ritual or through direct mystical experience.

WHY VALUES ARE IMPORTANT

Values carry our promise and our possibilities. They provide the intangible income we derive from our work and our play. Values related to citizenship, democracy, and sharing in our public trust also inform both work and life. On the other hand, the absence of values leaves us with nothing but trivial pursuits. Without values, life is empty and vulgar, without sources of meaning.

Interests, skills, and values are critical aspects of the self at work. As Clarifier, the parent is giving legitimacy to the existence and importance of these aspects of the child's emerging self-concept. Fostering the growth of interests, skills, and values is perhaps the core of the self-assessment support provided by the parent. One of the best exercises for surfacing values is asking your child to write her obituary—the one she wants to appear at the end of her life, decades from now. How old would she want be: seventy, eighty, ninety? What would she want to have accomplished? Help her to fantasize about what she might achieve and attain by the middle of the twenty-first century, to project beyond her immediate limitations, to stretch. This exercise helps to focus on the values and the skills she will acquire, apply, share, and create for herself.

ASSESSING PERSONALITY—MERGER OF SELF AND WORK

Most developmental models of career growth see the highest stage of growth related to a merger of self and career where work becomes a form of self-expression. At one level, we might say that is nice when people get to do what they want. But there is a deeper truth here than just a delight in doing your own thing.

To some extent, we all want to erase the line between work and play. The focus of most career counseling is helping the individual to identify work that is a natural expression of personality. *Personality* is one of those difficult words with many meanings. Here we use it to refer to the process of bringing together a coherent sense of self.

THE MYERS-BRIGGS TYPE INDICATOR (MBTI) ASSESSMENT

One of the most useful measures of personality comes from the *Myers-Briggs Type Indicator* (MBTI) personality inventory. Career application of the MBTI assessment has become increasingly sophisticated and represents one of the most successful tools for gathering self-assessment data. Helping your child get access to the MBTI assessment and to some of the books about the vocational interpretation of it is a fast start in understanding the role of personality in career decision making. (See the Parent Tool Kit section for specific ideas. Two standout books are *Do What You Are* by Tieger and Barron-Tieger [2001], which provides detailed career suggestions by MBTI type and *Are You My Type?* by Wirths and Bowman-Kruhm [1992], which introduces the concept of personality typing to young people.)

The MBTI assessment developed out of the work of Carl Jung and represents a most effective effort to identify personality type, which is very important to career decision making. Type is determined by the interaction of a cluster of preferences that lie behind much of our decision process. Jung argued that these preferences are a part of our nature, rather than something we learn. Though environmental factors help build our personality, type theory suggests that we have natural preferences for how we become energized, take in information, make decisions, and live our lives. These preferences are organized into four pairs of opposites, or dichotomies, as described in Chart 7.

We all use both sides of each of these four dichotomies. The idea of the MBTI instrument is to try to assign a relative weight to our preferences. Though there are no right or wrong preferences (just as use of one hand is no better than use of the other), there is effective and ineffective behavior. For example, a very strong preference for Judging can lead to rigidity and inflexibility, whereas a very strong preference for Perceiving can lead to inability to make and keep commitments. These possible weaknesses are not the result of some character defect. Rather, they arise from the preference of Judging types to put away decisions and not consider them further once closure is achieved, and the orientation of Perceiving types to see the constant parade of new opportunities that come into view.

THE MBTI° ASSESSMENT AND CAREER CHOICE

We use both sides of each dichotomy in any vocational situation. What research has shown is that working from our non-preferred side takes more energy than working from our

CHART 7	**Extraversion (E) and Introversion (I): E–I Dichotomy** We tend to gather our energy from the outer world of people and things (preference for Extraversion) or the inner world of ideas (preference for Introversion). A preference for Extraversion indicates that we receive energy from external events, experiences, people. A preference for Introversion indicates that we get energy from time spent with thoughts, inner awareness, reflections on events.

OVERVIEW OF MBTI® PREFERENCES

Extraversion (E) and Introversion (I): E–I Dichotomy We tend to gather our energy from the outer world of people and things (preference for Extraversion) or the inner world of ideas (preference for Introversion). A preference for Extraversion indicates that we receive energy from external events, experiences, people. A preference for Introversion indicates that we get energy from time spent with thoughts, inner awareness, reflections on events.

Sensing (S) and Intuition (N): S–N Dichotomy We gather data through our senses, seeing what is there, or we use our intuition to visualize all possibilities and relationships. Simply put, people with a preference for Sensing will focus on the visible in life, and people with a preference for Intuition will look at those invisible but real connections that exist in any event.

Thinking (T) and Feeling (F): T–F Dichotomy We think our way through decisions using reason, or we feel our way through decisions using our values. Within most business organizations, research has shown that people with a preference for Thinking will view people with a preference for Feeling as willing to sacrifice justice for harmony. In turn, Feeling types will view Thinking types as sometimes insensitive to the emotional content of the decision, how different people will feel about the outcomes. Thinking types are in search of an objective standard for truth. Feeling types look to how much they care about a choice, how much they value the different outcomes.

Judging (J) and Perceiving (P): J–P Dichotomy If we prefer to gather data (Perceiving preference), we may avoid getting to closure on a decision (Judging preference). If we get to closure too quickly, we may be ignoring important data. A preference for Perceiving indicates a desire in most situations to continue to gather data or information and continue the discussion rather than make a final decision. Perceiving types will reopen decisions their Judging type colleagues consider settled and closed. They will report that they are plagued by second thoughts once a decision is made and that they see too many possibilities in any given situation.

preferred side. For instance, a person with a strong preference for Introversion (I) who gets into sales (more of an Extraverted occupation) will use up so much energy dealing with people that she risks burnout if she does not give herself enough alone time to recharge her batteries. A person with a strong preference for Extraversion (E) in the same job will likely be energized by the contact with other people. If a corporate culture is ESTJ (as many manufacturing and engineering firms are), the INFP person working there will use up energy simply trying to be in the mainstream of the organization, whereas the ESTJ person will feel energized by all the like-minded people.

The personality can undergo many transformations across a life span because it is not static. Yet the personality is stable. Certain core descriptions of personality are more or less familiar to most of us: Are we Introverted or Extraverted? Are we orderly and logical in our approach to life, or are we spontaneous and intuitive? How much confidence and curiosity do we possess? Are we intentional in setting goals and taking action to reach those goals? Do we balance our needs with those of the group? Do we build relationships and enjoy intimacy and community? The personality comprises such basic orientations, but the total is greater than the sum of the parts. As much as we might want to break down personality into its constituent parts, it remains a somewhat mysterious whole.

What vocational psychologists have discovered in the last half-century is that certain work environments tend to attract and reward certain personalities. Corporations often hire clinical psychologists with training in assessment to help identify those personalities that thrive in their particular corporate culture. As parents helping our children with self-assessment, we help them think about personality and make the connection between personality type and work environment. The successful job candidate is the one who connects best, fits best with the organization.

EMOTIONAL INTELLIGENCE—HANDLING OUR PASSIONS

Joseph Campbell, the great mythologist, thought the best career advice was to follow your bliss. The problem is that following your bliss is not always blissful.

Joseph Campbell, the great mythologist, thought the best career advice was to follow your bliss. The problem is that following your bliss is not always blissful. Part of the self-assessment process is understanding our own emotional intelligence, our awareness of our emotions and how to control them, the ability to handle anger, rejection, injustice, discrimination, hatred. To control instinctive hostility and make it work for us, rather than allowing it to control us and make us work for it, is a major objective of growing our emotional intelligence.

The emotional network within the brain operates on the principle of association. Certain events of the past trigger behavior in the present. If we touch a red-hot stove, we learn not to do so again by associating the red, glowing stove with the burning sensation of scared flesh. However, students of autobiographical memory are pointing to possibilities of learning and unlearning certain emotional responses. Because our emotional networks fire off virtually instantaneously, all humans need discipline and control, especially under conditions of stress and exhaustion. The act of thinking takes a little longer than do our emotional responses. Some of the lessons of emotional intelligence have to do with building buffers between our emotions and our actions. We all know we should count to ten or one hundred before acting on anger. Similarly, we can learn how to deflect our anger from the immediate situation. Developing the discipline and the self-control to do that—and thereby to grow and change—is in part what we mean by *emotional intelligence*.

Daniel Goleman (1997) outlines the need for families, communities, schools, and religious organizations to take seriously our ability to grow our behavior controls, to grow in our ability to defer gratification. The use of violence to get what we want represents emotional stupidity; instead we can fight against negative thinking, emotional reactions, and behaviors triggered by events in the past and learn to manage our emotions, control impulses, delay gratification, read social cues, and cope with situations that prompt a negative response. That same growth promotes empathy—our ability to understand the emotional states and behaviors of others.

As Goleman points out, the development of emotional intelligence in children begins well before they enter school. In fact, Goleman found that success in school depends to a large extent on emotional characteristics that are formed in the years preceding entry into school. In his studies of successful people in a wide variety of career fields, Goleman found that whereas those with high IQs do very well, those within that group who also score high in emotional intelligence have an extra competitive edge. Those with extra doses of emotional intelligence—which includes the ability to build rapport, to show empathy, to build consensus, and to generally control one's own impulses and anger—possess the qualities that lead to real success. Unfortunately, these very qualities are found in ever-diminishing supply.

Thus, parents who wish for their child's success can begin when the child is very young to act as an emotional coach and mentor. Although the roles described in this book of Clarifier, Connector, Challenger, and Motivator have direct application when the child enters early adolescence and begins the process of defining himself in vocational terms, the role of emotional coach can begin years earlier. As Goleman states, "Having emotionally intelligent parents is itself of enormous benefit to a child."

In the workplace of the future, people with high levels of emotional intelligence will have an even greater advantage. The old model of manager as jungle fighter is a symbol of the corporate world's past; those who have strong interpersonal skills will be the leaders of the future. In all respects, ranging from the ability to work effectively with people of diverse backgrounds to being able to listen well and motivate people, those with emotional intelligence will succeed. Parents can do few things that will assist their children other than equipping them with these qualities. Not directly tied to career choice, it is nevertheless a gift that children will appreciate, regardless of what direction their careers take them.

Emotional intelligence is an important concept for children to understand. In the same way we learn certain historical facts, we can learn about emotions and their control, and begin to understand our own motivation. Propensities to aggressiveness or self-destructiveness are patterns that, left unchecked, become part of our neurological wiring, and puberty is a time when neural foundations are being formed, when self-consciousness is taking shape.

Self assessment is a critical part of the process of making life decisions—about drugs, violence, sex, cultism, education, family, career. The purview of this book is career and work, but the wider implications of the growth of emotional intelligence cannot be underestimated. In a world where we are all connected by an instantaneous electronic neural system, television's live images of hatred, brutality, and genocide can spawn destructive passions around the globe. Five hundred years ago, new ideas and technologies might have taken one hundred years to circulate, the slowness of dissemination providing a psychological buffer. Now we have no time to adjust to new knowledge or to the volume of technological change. Each of us has a meaning system that adjusts to new information, and that system is now barraged with more data in a year than past generations absorbed in a lifetime.

However, because our habits are built through actions, if we do principled and productive actions over and over again, we will lead principled and productive lives. Despite the assaults on our emotional intelligence, we can help our children learn how to handle distress and impulse by teaching correct actions. We can legitimize the learning of a neural architecture that will support lifetime preferences for mercy, justice, balance, a positive attitude toward life, and respect

QUESTIONS TO ASK

YOUR CHILD

THE PARENT AS CLARIFIER

- Are there things that you really enjoy spending time reading about or thinking about or doing, that fascinate you so much that you would want to devote your working hours to them?

- What are some skills you have that you would like to utilize in your career?

- What will be most important to you in making a career choice, knowing that you will probably have to make some trade-offs?

for behavioral norms. Honesty, personal responsibility, and loyalty to a social order larger than the individual are learned behaviors that combat violence, hatred, and prejudice.

In helping the child with self-assessment, parents are modeling behaviors they use in their own lives. In the career decision–making process, we have a prototype of what it means in one area of life, our work, to examine ourselves, our motives and our actions, and to understand the consequences of action. By careful examination of interests, skills, values, personality, and emotional intelligence, the child learns what thoughts and feelings are guiding and shaping a decision, that decisions do not just happen but are the outcome of a process and a variety of factors, many of which can be changed or altered if desired. Above all, self-assessment is a rational process that introduces intentionality into what otherwise might be experienced as magic or chance.

GEORGE'S STORY

George was a highly sensitive student who excelled in the sciences. His parent-teacher conferences usually centered on the teachers' concerns that George was "high-strung" and very introverted. George's father, Jim, wanted to press George into extraverted activities where George could demonstrate leadership potential that would allow him to enter the same high-paying sales work as Jim. "Like father, like son" was the thinking that guided this career development strategy. Jim functioned as Clarifier by motivating George to engage in tasks even if George resisted. When George did not show natural aptitude or interests in these activities, Jim and his wife, Mary Barbara, had the wisdom to back off and support George in activities he himself enjoyed and at which he excelled.

George loved spending time on his computer, and battles would rage with Jim over the size of the telephone bill. Jim knew George loved

being online, but he could not figure out a way to help George use this aptitude for career discovery. Because of poor hand-eye coordination, George did not do well in childhood team sports. He did enjoy running long distances and in high school came under the influence of a track coach who got George interested in the cross-country team and in training on his own for the local marathons. Jim would support George by attending every 10K race George entered, and they worked together on plans to finance George's running in the Boston marathon.

Jim found that the guidance professionals at George's middle school were not funded to provide the *Strong Interest Inventory*, MBTI, or other assessment tools. Jim read in a magazine article that the National Board for Certified Counselors (910-547-0607) had a referral service, as did the American Counseling Association (703-823-9800). Using these services, he was able to find a qualified career counselor who met with George and administered the *Strong*. The *Strong* suggested what Jim and George already knew:

George had very focused career interests in the Investigative Theme and high correlation with individuals employed in computer-related fields. This information served as a helpful compass in finding the first direction in career exploration. The counselor also provided a useful list of career-related Web sites.

Jim took the time to share the Internet interest and with George he visited the many Web sites with vocational information. George used the Web-Crawler (http://webcrawler.com/select/bus.employment.html) to help add to the counselor's list of sites. At one site (http://www.espan.com/docs/oohand.html), they were able to look at the *Occupational Outlook Handbook* published by the Bureau of Labor Statistics. There Jim was shocked to learn that Webmasters, the professionals who maintain the 250,000+ Web sites that George enjoyed browsing, earn between $50,000 and $100,000 a year.

Jim's support and interest helped George clarify his career interests and actually identify a career direction in Web site construction and multimedia authoring.

KEY ACTIONS

THE PARENT AS CLARIFIER

- Watch for natural interests and support their development.

- Provide an environment rich in opportunities for your child to express interests and preferences.

- Have your child complete an interest inventory.

- Legitimize the development of natural skills that may or may not have commercial potential.

- Give legitimacy to the existence and importance of interests, skills, and values as aspects of your child's emerging self-concept.

- Help your child think about personality and make the connection between personality type and work environment.

- Help your child learn how to handle distress and impulse, to develop emotional intelligence.

- Review with your child the data from his or her self-assessment (interests, skills, values, personality type), and keep the focus on the child as the key player in the process.

5

IDENTIFYING AND EXPLORING OPTIONS

PARENT AS CONNECTOR

> *In the end, it is the child's responsibility to make the career decision with the parent's support.*

IN THE CAREER EXPLORATION PHASE, the parent's role is to make connections. There are more than 10,000 entries in the *Dictionary of Occupational Titles*, and parents cannot know about them all. Even the most accomplished career counselor will have areas of in-depth knowledge and other areas of relatively superficial understanding. However, what both parents and counselors must do is involve the child, thereby encouraging growth and learning. In the end, it is the child's responsibility to make the career decision with the parent's support. We hope it is liberating to know that you as parent do not have to come up with the answers, just clarify questions. Besides, sound guidance rarely takes the form of easy answers.

MATCHING SELF-ASSESSMENT TO CAREER OPTIONS

Decision making is a learned skill. At this stage of learning, our concern is to help the child gather sufficient data about the real world of work to eventually make an informed career decision.

We suggested that you start the career coaching process by quite deliberately gathering data about the self because decisions are keyed to the self—to making and keeping commitments, to managing expectations, to learning how to predict logical outcomes of behavior, and to building a sense of responsibility, integrity, and self-esteem. Now comes the stage of moving your child into the world of work.

One of the truths discovered by modern psychology is that action precedes motivation: if we wait around to get motivated, we never act. When we act, we experience the rewards of our action, and that serves as motivation for future actions. The parent and teachers and counselors are all working to help the child feel enough personal power to take such action.

Career exploration is the domain in which the child builds hopes and trust. She learns to have hopes for a specific future that she can construct, creating options for herself. She learns to trust in the process by which she is learning to make decisions. It is vastly more productive for the child to invest some time learning that a particular career is not for her than for you to tell her you think that career is a bad choice. Thus it is important that the child not think that you are contemptuous of her choices and ideas and that you play by her rules for a while, honoring her analytical process.

Consider telling your son or daughter, "You do some exploration and we can talk about what you find." This approach is much more effective in building self-confidence than ignoring the child's own conclusions or acting indifferent to what assessment tasks the child has undertaken. The role of Connector should be liberating because you do not need to act like an expert who knows all about all careers; in fact, that would be inappropriate. As you and your child talk, slowly a vision of the future should begin to emerge. The freedom you grant your child to make decisions is a foundation for the development of his own good judgment and understanding of other people. It is far more important for him to grow into being his own expert by gathering data, by making and sticking to little decisions on the way to larger decisions.

There are several ways to help your child access what she learned in thinking about herself—her skills, her values, her personality, her interests. The first way is to ask what counselors call *projective questions*, such as, "If you could wave a magic wand and do whatever you liked, what would you do?" This gives your child a chance to integrate data. A good follow-up is her own favorite question—Why? You can ask her, "Why did you choose that?" This gives you a sense of how your child is thinking. What kind of logic is she using to get from her own data to the world of work?

If you sense that money is a dominant concern, you might uncover your child's interests by asking, "If you won the lottery and had all the money you could want, what would you do?" Earning a good living for oneself and one's family is not an irrelevant value in a highly competitive market economy where it is tough simply to stay employed. However, here in the early stages of career exploration, the child needs to explore a variety of areas of potential vocation that are in keeping with his competitive nature, decisiveness, creativity, and ingenuity.

A second way to access data is to help the child actually prepare lists of interests, skills, values. For younger children, it is helpful to get them thinking in the future: "What are some skills you might like to have?" Interests are a little harder to get at. "How do I know if I am interested in that if I have never done it?" is not a bad question and is often asked even by adults when completing interest inventories such as the *Strong Interest Inventory* assessment.

Some forms for making lists of interests, skills, and values are included in Part Three. Working from the lists also gives the child a record, almost like a journal or diary, which can be instructive as a benchmark in showing how much change took place between puberty and adolescence. The brain is growing, and like any other part of the body it needs training, exercise, and understanding. In helping your child understand a concept like emotional intelligence, you help her demystify one of the most important parts of the body—the brain.

Whether you use projectives or lists or both, it is important to get your child to make some connections between his data and the world of work. What you want here is someplace to start gathering data. Be careful not to push for the direct connection between the self-assessment and the career world that is most logical to you. Children have marvelous contact with their intuition, which most of us adults have lost or squandered. If it looks to you like an intuitive leap, go with the child's insight. By valuing and respecting what he comes up with, you build his confidence in the process.

TO COLLEGE OR NOT TO COLLEGE?

The motivation to narrow down career options often starts when students begin to wonder what they will do after high school. For many parents and school administrators, the gauge of success is that they decide to go on to a four-year college. "I want Charlie to be the first one in the family to graduate from college." Surveys suggest that up to 85 percent of teens and parents think this is a good goal, and most secondary schools use this as a baseline indicator of school performance. Unfortunately, only about half of those teens will actually graduate from college within six years, and only 57 jobs will be available for every 100 degrees.

What's the problem? According to Kenneth Gray, author of *Getting Real: Helping Teens Find Their Future* (2000), *they go to college by default. They do not know what else to do. Deciding on what to do after high school should be based on a realistic assessment of individual likes and dislikes, as well as strengths and weaknesses as they relate to labor market opportunities. Success comes from planning, and that planning requires knowing the direction in which one wants to head. Today, teens go to college and sit back to see what will happen when it's over.*

This is why self-assessment is the critical first step before deciding on options, and why college should not be an assumed goal or a goal unto itself. The first question is, What do you want to be able to do? Once that is clear, How can you get there? is a more focused and meaningful question.

A four-year degree program certainly is an important option to consider, but so are formal apprenticeship programs, certificate programs, associate degree programs, military opportunities, and volunteer activities such as the Peace Corps. None should be automatically ruled in or out without considering how it might help meet the young person's interests, skills, values, and long-term aspirations. Otherwise, "they enter college not knowing where they are headed and they graduate the same way. Those who enroll in occupation-specific programs [are] statistically more likely to graduate" (Gray 2000).

That's not to say that there is not value in education for the sake of developing the basic skills discussed earlier: emotional intelligence, maturity, discipline, critical thinking, expanding one's view of the world. Liberal arts programs that promote these basic skills can be extremely valuable and foundational. Parents can support those types of college decisions while encouraging their children to continue the career planning and exploration processes—learning more about their career fields of interest—throughout their education journey rather than wait until the end and then wonder "Now what?" Ideally they will do much of this exploration prior to making costly postsecondary decisions.

LEARNING MORE ABOUT A CAREER FIELD OF INTEREST

Exploring a career field is, at any age, an incremental process with four levels of time commitment:

- Reading about the career

- Talking and networking with people in the career

- Finding short-duration employment or courses related to that career

- Finding longer-duration employment or training/education

A useful metaphor to explain this process is the planning process one might go through in thinking about spending the summer or semester abroad in a foreign country. Ask your child to think about what she would do if she were going to travel to another country she had never visited. She first might go to the library and read travel guides written by people who have been there. She might get on the Internet and see if that country's office of tourism has a home page or a Web site. She might go to the video store and rent some travelogues or documentaries on that country or region. Armed with the questions and knowledge gained from reading and viewing and surfing the Internet, she probably would try to find in her network of friends someone who had traveled in that country. She might want to take a short trip to the country herself before committing herself for the whole summer or semester. In the end, she has to make a decision about going for the longer duration.

CAREER READING

The local public library is often the best resource to investigate careers with your child. It is very useful to go with him, not to do the work for him but to share in the learning process. Look for books written about the career field by the professional association or labor union within that field or government publications such as the *Dictionary of Occupa-*

tional Titles or the *Occupational Outlook Handbook*, which are now online and can be accessed through your home computer. Ask the librarian for other references, such as the *Guide to Occupational Exploration* and *Real People, Real Jobs*. There are many other books about individual career fields written for the express purpose of career exploration.

It is a good idea to start with introductory books because they will give you access to a whole world of information available from associations and unions and educational institutions in the 17,000,000 Web sites on the World Wide Web, or other Internet gopher or usenet sites, or printed material your child can write for. If you use search engines such as Veronica and Web Crawler, you can find the most interesting career-related sites simply by searching the name of the career—e.g., accountant, neurologist, plumber, civil engineer, protective services.

In addition to this information, most books about the career field will also point to magazines, newsletters, and other periodicals. If your child shows real interest in a particular publication, you might consider helping her fund the cost of a year's subscription, especially if the magazine is not in the local libraries.

Although adolescents and young adults living at home probably do not need your company when doing basic research at the library, it is a good idea to set up a time to discuss what data on the career field has been surfaced and how it is being processed. Reading, done in the library or on the Internet, is always the first step, but it is done with the second step in mind.

TALKING AND NETWORKING

Your child's network process begins with her own eyes and ears in career exploration. Your network will be the first source of her network; your friends and acquaintances will be among the first people she will talk with as part of her career exploration. But she will soon need to grow her own network—drawing names from her reading, from her friends' parents, from teachers and others in her circle.

Most schools have career days when parents come to class and talk about their work, or the school sponsors field trips to work sites so children can learn about real people in real jobs. These kinds of experiences are helpful in getting the child to break the ice and go out to meet people on his own. They are also helpful in understanding the basic truth that work environments are different. This learning can then be applied by using books that explain the importance of the connection between personality types and work environments. Some work environments are discouraging and unpleasant for some people. Just coming to that clarity is a great moment in the career decision–making process.

When your child starts to talk with people, a lot of surprising information may come home for verification by you. The fundamental message children usually hear from people they interview is that the average tenure of most jobs is about two years and the average life of most careers is about seven years. Your child will learn quickly that even if she stays in the same job, that job will have changed in content, demands, and expectations.

Your child may come home with phrases such as *market driven* and *customer focused* and will want to know what they mean for his work. Once career exploration starts in earnest, so do the questions. Parents and teachers and counselors do not have all the answers. Mostly we just have more questions.

Let your child hear from you about your experience of jobs and careers. If she is concerned about the instability or insecurity, talk about it. If she is worried about ever getting a job, talk about that. What does a life spent working in an intensely competitive environment mean to her? What has it meant to you? What does it mean to work in organizations called flat, horizontal, hollow, virtual?

Vocational mobility is a frightening concept, but through talking with others about it and networking, your children will learn that it is a reality of the twenty-first century. Most of our kids have to become the multitalented, multifunctional workers of the future; to thrive in the new economy, they will need to reinvent themselves more or less continuously around a core vocational identity that is their source of integrity.

Through networking, your children may also pick up on the fact that employment security in their lifetime will be based on lifelong learning of new skills consistent with their core career motivations. The new mission statement of most employers will emphasize better technology, better production processes, and fewer, better workers. Your child, like you, like each of us, therefore needs to develop, in addition to basic skills, career-making expertise such as networking skills and self-marketing skills, which helps him move beyond his own barriers.

The new work environment will also demand the development of self-management skills. Your children will have to learn the art of quick follow-up. They must learn how to be a part of a global economy in which 50 percent of the new wealth created in the next ten years will be created in Asia. They will have to acquire a profound vendor orientation even if they are not in a sales function. They must act as if they have an ownership stake in the business at hand or they will not be working for long. Networking, learning to learn, and personal enterprise are the new success skills. By planning ahead and knowing which skills and attitudes they need, they will be ready to learn them at school, college, or place of employment.

In this new work environment, every individual needs to maximize her competence and commitments, her knowledge of the organization's product and work, her experience at coordinating her work with that of others inside and outside the organization, and finally her ability to motivate herself to do what needs to be done. This new environment is the very picture of freedom, but your child may see this freedom to be herself as frightening. If so, talk about it with her. The key skill is learning, building knowledge capital. Every job, every work assignment is an opportunity to learn new information, new technology, new skills, new discipline.

Talking and networking begin to put career information into the hands of your child. Career information is not only about what dentists or veterinarians or product placement specialists do; in a broader sense, it is also about the world of work. Your child needs both sets of data. In helping him network, get him to think about a script for the interview. What are the joys and frustrations of your work? What do you read to help you learn about new trends or directions in your field? What are the skills and interests you look for in someone who wants to get into this field? If your son wanted to make this his career, what advice would you give him?

Do not forget to teach the forgotten art of sending thank-you letters. This is a good time to learn about stationery and handwritten notes. If you have a home computer with software that will allow her to manage her own database, your child probably should learn how to manage her network, sending thank-you notes and periodic follow-ups indicating how she is doing.

Children question what they really want, what really interests them in light of what they are learning about the world.

The whole point of career exploration is to share the experience of those working in the field. This kind of vicarious experience, gathered through networking, forms a rational base from which your child can project his own reaction to the stresses and rewards of working in a particular field. The more data your child collects about the world of work, the more he is thrown back onto his own assessments of what he really wants. Children question what they really want, what really interests them in light of what they are learning about the world.

FINDING SHORT-DURATION EMPLOYMENT AND COURSES

From reading and talking with people, career exploration moves into gradual commitments of more time. Now we are looking for volunteer jobs, summer jobs, short-term internships, relevant courses, and workshops. These experiences yield further knowledge about the career and give your child an opportunity to test his competence.

The movement in this particular phase of the journey of self-discovery is from dualistic, static definitions of careers to the distant objective of viewing vocation as the accumulated commitments of a lifetime. In a sense, children need static categories to organize information about careers. Once they get to this level of commitment, they begin to experience the reality that careers are dynamic human events in which the individual defines the career as much as the career defines the individual.

In that movement toward new vision and new perspective, children need to learn that having problems is not a problem. Running away from problems or feeling sorry for ourselves because life is hard is the only real problem. Career growth is a type of life initiation that is or should be an adventure. Like most adventures, growing in our knowledge of careers and ourselves can be painful, but it is essentially joyful.

The parent as Connector helps the child to stay with his perceived hopes and trust in his vision of himself.

Too often, children can come to view career growth as a demonstration that they are incompetent because they feel pain and confusion as they confront developmental tasks and crises. In this phase of career exploration, our work as parents is helping our children come to see that pain and confusion are positive aspects of growth, that the only thing that is painless is staying in the same place, which is painless only temporarily.

The parent as Connector helps the child to stay with his perceived hopes and trust in his vision of himself.

FINDING LONGER-DURATION EMPLOYMENT

Sri Ramakrishna and Saint Francis de Sales used almost the same words to say that winds of grace are always blowing— our job is to set our sails and steer. The steering may be fragile, incomplete, even incompetent, but it can only improve with practice. At this phase of career exploration, parents are beginning to see the growing wisdom of the child as decision maker.

THE PARENT AS CONNECTOR

QUESTIONS TO ASK YOUR CHILD

- Of the career fields suggested by your self-assessment or by the inventories you took, which two or three do you want to find out more about?

- What do you think would be some good ways for you to get some firsthand experience in those fields of interest?

- Would you like my help in linking you up with some people I know from whom you could learn about your areas of interest?

- Shall we go to the library together and check out some books on several career fields?

Of course, taking the career decision–making journey does not exempt us from the realities of accidents, failures, betrayals, illness, luck. Your child will meet all kinds of people who will give all kinds of advice—some good, some bad, some that is unsettling—and you can offer your opinion on the difference. But in the end, permit her the freedom to decide for herself who is smart and who is not.

This process does not exempt our children from slipping on their doubts and fears. But it does make us aware of the barriers we construct for ourselves—all the layers of fear that hold us back, all those voices saying to us that we cannot do what we believe in. As children approach major commitments—military service, college, vocational training, first jobs—they probably will confront unanticipated consequences of their decisions. Children need to learn about changing direction in response to immovable barriers. They must learn to call on every conceivable resource. They learn how to do all this on their own—but with your presence and support.

We hope you and your child develop a deeper sense of family, of community based on the work you do together in this process. We want your child to understand that career exploration and self-exploration are both authentic experiences and are relevant to real-world decisions.

THE PARENT AS CONNECTOR

CLIFF'S STORY

VERY EARLY IN junior high school, Cliff was diagnosed with Attention Deficit Disorder (ADD). This neurological disorder required, in his case, the use of medication. The clinical psychologist who worked with him said that ADD would have to factor into any career planning Cliff did. The disorder would not go away.

The psychologist referred Cliff to a career counselor who had experience with clients with ADD. When his mother, Laurie, found out that the career counselor's fee was $75 per hour, she called the counselor to see if a payment schedule could be worked out. It could, so Laurie, who was a single parent, connected with the counselor and together they built a career exploration program.

Cliff had talked with Laurie and his grandmother, Donna, about many career possibilities, and they visited the library together to see what they could learn. This work in advance of the career counseling session helped focus the work Cliff and the counselor would do. He loved two things above all others—African American history and dogs. Although his ADD did not prevent him from looking at a career as a scholar and teacher of history, many of the tasks would prove demanding. His natural instinct for relating to the two family dogs—Hogan and Brahmin—seemed like an important aptitude to explore.

The career counselor suggested looking at the vocational world related to dogs, from veterinary science to professional dog handler to kennel management. Cliff had shown one of the family dogs at a match and enjoyed the experience but came in third in his breed class so thought he had no aptitude. The career counselor suggested looking at books and magazines related to dog breeding, training, exhibiting. Cliff and Donna returned to the library and found magazines such as *Dog World* and the *American Kennel Club Gazette,* which had advertisements for professional dog handlers, and they identified one that lived near them.

The career counselor had suggested a career exploration interview with professionals in the dog field, so Donna called the professional dog handler and asked if she and Cliff could come and visit to talk about the career. They met the handler, who explained the many factors that went into winning in the show ring. Cliff saw that he had been too quick in his judgment that he did not have the aptitude to be a good dog handler. The meeting was a success not only because of the information he got about the field but also because the handler was willing to set up an unpaid internship for weekend shows. Cliff continued his interest in dogs throughout high school, and by learning to cope with his ADD he went on to veterinary technician training.

KEY ACTIONS

THE PARENT AS CONNECTOR

- Help your child gather data about the real world at work.

- Honor your child's analytical process—it is vastly more productive for your child to invest time learning that a particular career is not for her than for you to tell her you think that career is a bad choice.

- You do not need to act like an expert who knows all about careers.

- Help your child connect the data gathered during self-assessment with various options, by asking, "If you could wave a magic wand and do whatever you liked, what would you do?"

- Connect your child to appropriate resources (reading, people, experiences) to assist with career exploration.

- Discuss the data your child finds and what he has learned from it.

- Connect your child to your network of friends and acquaintances for career exploration purposes.

- Help your child to see that pain and confusion are positive aspects of growth.

- Help your child to stay with her perceived hopes and trust in her vision of herself.

6

GOAL SETTING AND PLANNING

PARENT AS CHALLENGER

EMOTIONAL INTELLIGENCE ENABLES US to step back from a situation and choose appropriate emotional responses to our feelings and social situations. Each of us has the ability to choose happiness, anger, and joy to an extent that was thought impossible a generation ago. However, growth in ability to handle emotional content does not just happen by accident or genetic disposition. Wise parents work to challenge their children to choose and stick with learning experiences that promote a sense of competence in emotional effectiveness and socialization. Goal setting and planning are among such learning experiences.

Goals grow out of our interests, skills, values, opportunities, effectiveness. As parent, you challenge your child to pick up the scent of important career goals. To read, to observe, to drift intentionally, to wander, to travel alone—all have long been a formula for personal transformation, for individual growth and change. In the same way that those seeking deeper understanding often connect with mountains, the desert, or the sea, your child needs to connect with the world of work—a complex world of ceaseless change.

In the process of setting goals, we come to know ourselves. Virtually every cultural tradition holds among its central principles "know thyself." The ancient Greeks thought that advice was so important that they carved it on the doorway to the Oracle at Delphi. Knowing ourselves, the capacity for reflective self-awareness, is perhaps our greatest personal achievement, at least the one that is most important to career success. Making up one's mind, coming to a new level of self-awareness, demonstrates a seriousness about oneself and about life.

TALKING ABOUT CAREER GOALS

Talking with your child about her career goals is critical. Children are not exposed very often to real discussion with adults; some have never experienced much serious discourse among people trying to arrive at the truth. Simply talking, taking an interest, is the most important challenge we parents make to growth. By asking your child to do some thinking about career, you indicate that such thinking is important. By helping her ask, "What is supposed to happen in my career?" you lay the foundations for progress.

Although the career decision–making process provides a useful frame for the conversation about career goals, the conversation itself communicates the importance of setting goals. When your child understands that he can do anything, then selecting something becomes very difficult. The parent as Challenger is helping the child to stay with the work demanded in that difficult process.

CAREER VULNERABILITY

Especially in times of extreme vocational vulnerability, your child profits from having learned to dig out her own vocational self-understanding. She learns how to discover the purposes that drive her, the goals she dreams of, the challenges that frighten her. Those tentative and often fearful steps toward self are what you, as Challenger, are facilitating.

In a very real sense, all of us are now self-employed, with all its attendant joys and fears. We all need to be doing work we want to do, work that uses our abilities and talents in meaningful ways.

In a time when every job is vulnerable, some people are identifying more completely and more devoutly with their current job. That is a faulty strategy according to accomplished career warriors, who warn that the more you try to hang on to your job, the more likely you are to lose it. When your child's career comes crashing down around his head, his lack of life diversity and a source of identity rooted in his employment rather than in himself puts him at serious psychological risk.

In a very real sense, all of us are now self-employed, with all its attendant joys and fears. We all need to be doing work we want to do, work that uses our abilities and talents in meaningful ways. The best career advice is now, and always has been, to find someone to pay you to do what you love doing. Yet doing what we love is not always possible. There are tensions and tradeoffs in every employment setting. Children are not immune to contradictions and dilemmas, but they can learn how to live more comfortably with those tensions. A review of the career decision–making process has much to teach us about living through layoff, relocation, reorganization, downsizing. The vocational vulnerability of the present day is our children's future.

PARENT-CHILD DIFFERENCES

Children are often attentive to what they are doing in the moment, caught up in the miracle of being alive. We parents have been alive for some time and perhaps have gotten a little jaded about the event. Thus we often get fixated on not wasting time, on moving ahead with a decision as quickly as possible. But even high achievers need to recognize that some of their actions are taken for their own rewards, just as your child smells the flowers and observes their beauty as an end in itself.

When we think about work and being at work, we forget that work can be fun. We are too busy to have fun, bobbing and weaving in a competitive environment. The secret that children often teach parents is that individual tasks in our work are ends in themselves. Yes, taken together they do meet some larger goal, but children often realize intuitively that life is about enjoying what you do. For that reason, a child can often see that doing forty things you do not like doing to achieve a goal you *do* like does not make sense. For children, the means are the ends.

The parent as Challenger needs to remember these important differences between adults and children. If something or someone is obstructing their joy, children work on that obstacle and try to create change for the better; they have a kind of natural instinct to reduce suffering, especially their own. In challenging the development of goals, we parents need to remember some childhood wisdom.

SETTING MEANINGFUL GOALS

The goal of effective career decision making is to discover the ways in which your child can be nourished by work. Those discoveries happen over a lifetime. To make those discoveries, we need to think about our personal goals.

GOAL-SETTING SKILLS

Children learn that when we form commitments to certain principles, we then are called upon to act with integrity — that is, to act consistently with our values and hopes, to put our skills into practice. We all struggle to adjust our way of life to our value commitments. In making career decisions, children are struggling to develop clarity of purpose. They aim for certain goals and do what they need to do to achieve those goals. They then find out for themselves that the gap between willing and doing is huge.

Learning to set goals and objectives is a skill in itself. Chart 8 describes an easy method of setting goals. College students often report that parental goal-setting skills and habits had the greatest influence on their own habits. In career decision making, goals refer to short-term personal performance goals in the activities of career exploration, self-assessment, taking action. As Challenger, the parent is helping the child set a reasonable agenda for action. For instance, a child returns from a career exploration interview in which she was told that a really gifted student who devotes about twenty years of intense study and work can hope to reach the first stage of proficiency in this career. In such a case, the Challenger may help the child to see that this advisor probably has an inflated opinion of himself and his work. But they then may help their child to set some realistic milestones that could be set to be reached along the way.

The key question in any goal-setting activity is, "What are we trying to accomplish here?" Your interest as parent in what the child is trying to accomplish is the start of effective goal setting. Goals focus your child's attention on the process involved in career decision making, which is itself designed to mobilize action, energies, and efforts. By getting the child to sign on to work at the process, to work toward specific goals, you increase the potential that she will stick with the task—whatever that task is. Setting goals and taking steps to achieve them should both involve your child.

In career decision making, each stage and substage of the process is designed to provide feedback to all the other stages. Clarity of career direction becomes its own reward. The more career exploration activities that take place, the more likely it is that the child gains in self-awareness. Knowing which

CHART 8

SETTING "SMART" GOALS

An easy way to remember how to set meaningful goals, used in corporate business planning sessions, is to remember that a good goal is a *SMART* goal:

Specific

Measurable

Attainable

Results-focused

Time-framed

- Goals should identify as *specific* a direction as possible. For example, encourage your child to go beyond the statement "I'd like to get into business" by questioning what aspects of business interest him or her: marketing? finance? manufacturing? human resources?

- How will the goal be measured, or how will your child know when he or she has succeeded? An example of a *measurable* goal might be, "In ten years I would like to be working as a partner in a law firm" or, "By the time I am forty years old, I want to have published two books."

- Although we have continually encouraged you to help your children reach for their potential, to challenge themselves to look beyond the obvious or easy way out, a critical aspect of goal setting is to discuss the *attainability* of the aspirations. Stretch goals are good, but milestones take them beyond a dream toward potential reality.

- Focusing on *results* rather than activities helps keep the end objective in sight. "I'm going to go to college" can be replaced with "I'm going to earn a degree in education so that I can become a high school teacher."

- Finally, though *time frames* will no doubt change along the way, timelines help guide the process of reaching goals as well as assessing progress along the way. What does your child want to be doing in five years? Ten? Twenty? What does he or she want to accomplish in his or her lifetime?

career directions he does not want to take helps to focus on directions he might want to take.

GOAL-SETTING CHALLENGES

Children struggle with the diversity of career possibilities. It is a jolt for them to meet and talk with people in the same career with very different perspectives on that career field. Children need to learn that different commitments and different values exist for each of us in a culture of flux.

Goals need to be both specific and challenging. How high you set them is a matter for negotiation between you and your child.

Facilitating goal setting and commitment is one of the important contributions you can make.

Your involvement in helping to set goals also helps to overcome resistance to commitment. Your presence in the process supports the child and deters him from quitting the process before a critical amount of self-awareness has taken shape. Facilitating goal setting and commitment is one of the important contributions you can make.

SPECIFIC GOAL-SETTING APPROACHES

In facilitating goal commitment, you need to minimize the effect of several impediments. First, your child will not subscribe to goals she does not believe she has the ability to accomplish. Her self-confidence is based on her belief in her competency to accomplish the tasks at hand (Brown & Lent 1996). In the case of career exploration interviews, she may not feel comfortable asking questions or writing the script or protocol of questions that make for confidence in handling the interview. Using some of the questions suggested in the section on career exploration interviews, let her interview you or a neighbor or close friend. The safety of familiarity and the practice she gets will help her get the motivation needed to carry off the project of seeing five or six people in one of the fields she has chosen to explore.

PERSONAL GOAL SETTING

Dr. David Campbell of the Center for Creative Leadership in Greensboro, North Carolina, studied the lives of successful people over fifteen years as part of a longitudinal study. He focused specifically on people who were leading the kinds of lives they wanted to lead and found some common characteristics in the way this group approached goal setting. First, he found that this group of people set goals for themselves that were right for them—goals based on their skills and abilities and an overall good sense of who they were. In addition, he discovered the following themes related to the goals these successful people set:

1. They repeatedly demonstrated a sense of planfulness and had developed a sense of where they wanted to go and set goals for themselves to get there.

2. The goals they set were flexible, as opposed to fixed or static. Due to the amount of change in the world, static goals often lead to disappointment. This was found to be true where parents wanted to pass on a goal to their children, only to find that the goal was no longer appropriate given the changing conditions.

3. The goals were renewable, rather than an end point. Goals that were not renewable led to a feeling of "Is this all there is?" once achieved.

4. The goals were established in such a way as to provide choices and options in the future, so that people did not get locked into some narrow path. Successful people were constantly doing things in the present to increase their options in the future.

5. There are certain assets that tend to increase one's options: one's skills (especially one's communications skills, which open many pathways) and one's motivation level, which ranges from the low end of doing what someone else makes you do (e.g., parents) to a high level of motivation, which results from adaptation, in which an individual adapts the organization to meet her needs. Other assets that can increase one's options in life included family and friends who can open doors (see Chapter 5 in this book); creativity, or the ability to see things differently; finances; appearance; and health.

Adapted from an audiotape on "Personal Goal Setting," from the book by David Campbell *If You Don't Know Where You're Going, You'll Probably End Up Somewhere Else,* 1994

Second, you need to monitor progress, help your child process what she is learning, and give her feedback. If your child sets a goal of five interviews, you need to talk with her after the first and the second to see how things are going. Did she get the information she needed and wanted? Did she learn anything about herself or her interests? Did she get excited or disenchanted about aspects of the career field? Were there any surprises? Did she learn things she wishes she hadn't, issues that might discourage her interest in the field?

FUNCTIONING AS INTERPRETER AND SUPPORTER

One of the important concerns and correctives you as Challenger bring to the process is helping your child learn to interpret what she is hearing. For instance, she may have an interview with a friend of one of her teachers, someone you do not know. In that interview, she finds the person is very depressed about the field and constantly says, "Why would you want to get into this career—it is a terrible career." The information your child gets is nothing but a litany of complaint. You need to help her filter out the negativity and understand that it is unhelpful for people who hate their work to give career exploration interviews to young persons, but they do, and the experience is one she may encounter again.

Being attentive, reflecting feelings, listening, and talking with your child is the foundation of your role as Challenger. The art of kindness is often lost in all the demands on our time.

Another problem children face is deciphering figurative language and jargon. It is embarrassing to the child to stop the interview repeatedly to ask the meaning of words being used. Many times you can help translate meanings, and the next interview will be more productive.

One of the areas in which parents see their role as Challenger most clearly is getting the child to keep working, to keep interviewing, to keep exploring after a bad experience. For instance one mother, whose daughter had read extensively about medicine and devoted herself to six or seven career exploration interviews and two days making rounds with women MDs, thought that career clarity had been won. The daughter, with great anticipation and excitement, landed a summer job in a hospital—with a boss who proceeded to harass the young woman sexually, thereby souring her on medicine. In addition to supporting her in the trauma and the legal questions, the mother successfully challenged the daughter to reinvent her career dream despite one very real nightmare.

Third, throughout the career decision–making process you can help provide the resources your child needs to reach his goals. Those resources include ideas, contacts, financing. You can help your child secure the expertise needed to break through a logjam in self-assessment and exploration to find educational internships that blend industry experience and the building of functional expertise. The most important contribution you make is your own time and interest. Being attentive, reflecting feelings, listening, and talking with your child is the foundation of your role as Challenger. The art of kindness is often lost in all the demands on our time.

ESTABLISHING SPECIFIC GOALS AND NEXT STEPS

The purpose of setting goals is to focus resources and activity in one area of endeavor. The focus of the career decision–making process is to formulate a hypothesis—"I like career X"—and then test that hypothesis through direct experience. We cannot overstate the importance of direct experience—reading, interviewing, courses, workshops, seminars, internships, summer jobs, volunteer work, temping. Any plan benefits from measurable results and forging links between research and action. Get the plan and the action steps up on the wall where they can remind you and your child of what she is trying to accomplish.

CAREER CHOICES IN TODAY'S WORLD

For many of us, career choice was largely a matter of serendipity, the art of making happy discoveries by accident. Actually what probably happened in most baby boomer career development was discovering what we did best and sticking with it. Direction, purpose, focus are the sources of career success, and many times those skills developed by accident. But that may be a luxury in the future. Unlike you, your child will have to develop skills and make purposeful decisions.

Children of the twenty-first century need to focus on what skills they like to exercise, what skills they do best. Getting a computer and putting your child online may be the best career exploration investment you can make. In developing an action plan, remember that skills exploration is vital. Children need the opportunity to explore what they might be good at. School is usually the vehicle for a lot of that exploration, and the secondary school curriculum—both academic and extracurricular—is usually the most influential point of exposure to skills: quantitative, mathematical, social, influential, ideational, musical, linguistic, kinesthetic, spatial, artistic, problem solving.

THE CHILD'S RATE OF PROGRESS

One of the problems parents confront is hanging onto the child's coattails as interest and skill exploration take place at the speed of light. Interest in photography leading to building a darkroom in the basement, which two months later is abandoned, can be frustrating. Help your child to think and act incrementally, to make some personal investment in the action plan. If the cost and responsibility are taken on by the child, that is a good measure of the level of interest and is an important part in building commitment.

"I want to try this" evolves into "I want to do this," which eventually evolves into "I need to do this." That evolution is the hope of every action plan in the career decision—making process.

What your child is searching for is the work, the exercise of skills, without which she cannot thrive. "I want to try this" evolves into "I want to do this," which eventually evolves into "I need to do this." That evolution is the hope of every action plan in the career decision–making process.

Careers are inherently personal and social artifacts. They arise from our innermost self, yet they are expressed in opportunities mediated by the society. For that reason, the career decision–making process requires exploration both of the self and of the work environment, the socially mediated phenomenal fields we label *careers*, such as computer technology, hospitality management, and entertainment promotion. Once the child understands the cognitive concept of

**QUESTIONS TO ASK
YOUR CHILD**

THE PARENT AS CHALLENGER

- What type of work can you imagine yourself doing in five years?

- How can your unique interests and talents be channeled into work?

- How many informational interviews have you completed?

- Are you going to apply for that internship opportunity at school?

congruence between self and work environment, action plans become much easier to develop.

CREATING ACTION PLANS

Action plans outline what your child plans and hopes to accomplish and by what date. If your child feels disorganized and has nothing to do, he will do nothing. The action plan is a meeting place for you and him to communicate about what is happening and what is hoped for. The action plan also provides a graphic representation of the parts of the career decision process he is working on. It is very important to get the action plan charted. Make a checklist of all the steps necessary to meet a specific goal, and decide on a date by which each step will be completed.

Working from a chart or a checklist helps the child grasp how one breaks down goals into specific steps. Monumental goals often seem so overwhelming that the child's motivation is crushed by the enormity of the task in front of her. But she needs to be reminded that the pyramids were built one step at a time. Creating action plans allows you to model effectiveness to your child. After all, you would not ask your children to do their own laundry or vacuum their room without some instruction. The same is true with more complex life tasks such as career decision making. Decision making is learned behavior: children need to be taught how to make decisions efficiently and effectively.

CAROL'S STORY

Carol loved the outdoors. She could wander through fields and woods losing all track of time. She would stop for hours and admire a wildflower or contemplate a newfound plant. Her parents were classic sixties hippies who believed anyone's highest calling was discovering his own destiny. Carol believed that too but could not seem to get a handle on what destiny looked like.

School was like prison for Carol. She could not wait to get outside, control her own time and tasks, become one with her natural surroundings. The school building itself seemed stagnant, out of touch with the flow of reality. She was involved with sports year-round and lettered every year of high school in three different sports. Financial cutbacks in the school district meant that student athletes had to pay for their own equipment and contribute to the fund for travel to away events. Carol and her team-

mates worked to raise money to support the team. Her work in sports made her popular, but she felt distanced from the career plans her friends were making.

By the end of her junior year of high school, Carol knew she was not ready for college. Her parents were both graduates of Ivy League colleges, but they did not push for a college decision. They did want her to make some kind of decision about her plans after high school, so they sat down with the guidance counselor, who was also Carol's basketball coach. Working together, they came up with a plan to get Carol into a career planning course the counselor was offering as an elective for seniors. The course was designed to get the student to investigate five different career options. Using the *Strong Interest Inventory* assessment as a compass to establish some basic directions, Carol found she had scored very high in the Realistic and Social themes as well as occupations related to teaching, community service, and parks and recreation.

Carol's parents had chosen simplicity as a lifestyle and did not have the funds

to send Carol to summer camp or Outward Bound. But they thought that working in a camp with special needs might be something Carol wanted to do. A friend of a friend operated such a camp and they arranged for her to visit the camp. It was one of life's illuminating experiences. Much of the camp's curriculum had been influenced by recent scholarship in adventure education, and Carol saw that she was meant to be an adventure educator.

One of her father's college classmates was a trainer in a company providing team-building courses to industry. Carol went to see her and with her help made contact with several other people in the field. It became clear that the kind of job Carol wanted would require a college degree eventually, but everyone she met wanted to give her an entry-level "gofer" position. She took a job with a year-round facility in North Carolina and a year after high school entered college with the idea of majoring in psychology.

KEY ACTIONS

THE PARENT AS CHALLENGER

- Talk with your children about career aspirations. Express interest in their plans, communicate the importance of setting goals.

- Provide resources such as ideas on how to get more information and contacts for informational interviews.

- Don't let them get discouraged if they are not excited about a field that they explore. Explain that clarifying what one does not want to do is an important step toward focusing on a direction they might want to take.

- Build self-confidence: brainstorm informational interview questions, let them practice asking them, give them feedback and suggestions.

- Discuss informational interview results with them. Decipher jargon that they hear from others; motivate them to move on if they've had a bad experience. Help them interpret what they are hearing and determine next steps.

- Help them monitor progress toward goals, process what they are learning, provide feedback and suggestions about how to keep or get back on track.

- Together create and review action plans, checklists, and milestones.

SUCCESS AND FAILURE AS LEARNING TOOLS

Career decision–making skill is similar to learning a lifetime sport. Anyone who has driven across the country with young children knows the human truth that absence of physical activity heightens emotional responses to ordinary events. Coop the kids up, keeping them physically inactive, and you have emotional dynamite. Children, and most adults, need physical activity every day. We all need recess. When children think they are failures at sports, they forget they need the disciplined physical activity even if they are not playing competitively or preparing for a professional sports career. The

concept of failure creeps into a child's mind and is hard to dis-
lodge—ask any professional athlete or performing artist. Successful people usually attribute their success to learning how
to learn from mistakes, from failures. Failure is at the core of
the creative process. Trial and error is not the most efficient
learning behavior, but it is the most reliable. No child should
ever be satisfied just with success, or afraid of failure.

CHAPTER 7

TAKING ACTION

PARENT AS MOTIVATOR

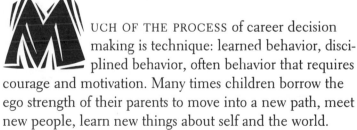

UCH OF THE PROCESS of career decision making is technique: learned behavior, disciplined behavior, often behavior that requires courage and motivation. Many times children borrow the ego strength of their parents to move into a new path, meet new people, learn new things about self and the world.

As Motivator, you are helping your child discover new paths to sustained high performance. You are also helping to overcome that charming nonchalance that so many children use to disguise a fear of failure. You may be motivating your child past thinly veiled disinterest; you may be motivating a child who systematically ignores all deadlines.

Sometimes the child goes off in a direction you want to discourage, but be careful about discouragement of a career that seems impractical and unimportant. Harvard scholar of education Jerome Bruner (1962) says that the shrewd guess, the fertile hypothesis, the courageous leap to a tentative conclusion—these are the most valuable coins of the thinker at work. Your child may try to break free from career by rote and take a direction she feels is unique to her. The career decision–making process requires that your child be freed—and burdened—to make her own choices, to enhance her own capacity for learning and change.

THE ART OF MOTIVATING

Throughout the career decision–making process, parents motivate behavior. Parents motivate children both to learn the process and to do the process. Motivating children is an art: just because we have known sorrow and fear and loss and failure does not mean we know what words soothe and comfort and empower in such moments of our child's life.

Unfortunately, parents often idealize the attributes that contribute to human success and enforce mistake-proof behavior, trying to twist the child into something the child cannot be. We tend to visit the child with our own frustrated ambitions.

However, the art of motivating career decisions is, in part, helping your child understand the delicate balance between liberty and necessity that governs most of our lives. In other words, we have the freedom to choose, but our choices must conform to what is possible given our health, fortune, skills, interests, opportunities, and time and place in history.

DEALING WITH FEAR AND APATHY

Motivational meltdown has many faces: the cantankerous child refuses to compromise, such as the fourteen-year-old who announces she is going to be a drifter and wants nothing to do with a culture of sellouts and imitators. Her authenticity and spunk are to be applauded as long as she does not end up cynical, frustrated, and disenfranchised.

The more common issue is motivating the fearful child. Many people who complain at midlife of having made the wrong career choice were fearful and could not countenance a setback or mistake, letting their momentum be their only guide. Children expect positive outcomes: they are not jaded; they have not yet experienced a world where you often get fired the year you were most productive. Children expect they will be rewarded for their efforts, and when those rewards do not come, they need help to stay with the task. When career exploration interviews, for instance, seem to create more confusion than clarity about career goals, children need the parent as Motivator.

In some motivational schemes, there is usually a place for fear and punishment, but not in the career decision process. The threat that "If you do not do these career exploration interviews, you are going to be a failure" does not work well. In fact, getting angry about the lack of effort or progress your child is making is counterproductive.

The career decision–making process usually generates its own rewards in the form of more knowledge of self and the world of work, more clarity about future possibility, more excitement and energy about working in a particular field. Sometimes the parent can introduce rewards external to the tasks by showing interest, engaging in some shared recreation, or providing financial help to get certain tasks completed. However, buying your child's participation in career decision making is as limited a motivational ploy as fear and punishment.

High school and college counselors often put together groups of students who are engaging in the same career exploration or self-assessment tasks in order to gain the power of group motivation. Family group motivation is similarly useful: the child is not out there alone; there is a support group to which she will report progress and failure, joy and frustration, triumphs and adventures.

Groups also help children cope with a big problem in making career decisions—apathy, staying motivated. At one level, children are apathetic when they fail to sense—and fight against—the disorder in their lives. When children are in the grips of such apathy, performance opportunities and growth opportunities are ignored. Behaviors that are self-enhancing or other-enhancing never take place.

On another level, too many children no longer have confidence in the utility and value of working. This type of apathy can leave the child permanently uninvolved, on the noncareer couch watching the reruns of his life. He gets his identity from a T-shirt; has no goals; does not work to match his skills with his challenges, growing where necessary. He won't risk getting feedback about how he is doing in learning, exploring, or thinking about the future, and avoids the sacrifice and inconvenience required by career decision making. In such cases, apathy is an evasion of reality, not a reaction to it. Of course, it is fine to drift and observe as methods for gathering information during a defined period of time.

The best we as humans can do in making decisions is to take action, solicit feedback so we can identify mistakes, learn from the feedback we receive, try to do the action better by always repeating the learning process.

The best motivation comes from understanding that apathy is not a response as much as it is a value. Not deciding is a form of decision. If a child can be persuaded that life is replete with choices and she is making one that you find hard to accept, she might be persuaded to understand that if she flies by the seat of her pants, she has to expect some rips. The best we as humans can do in making decisions is to take action, solicit feedback so we can identify mistakes, learn from the feedback we receive, try to do the action better by always repeating the learning process. We learn to live with the environment rather than control it or pretend it isn't there. We concentrate on living each moment with ourselves and with each other.

One truth to teach the apathetic child is that action precedes motivation. If we wait to get motivated, we rarely find time and energy to do the task. There are times when we need to just do a task without waiting for motivation, without focusing on the reward. Until we make a commitment by taking action, we do not allow others or serendipity to help us. We see the happy coincidences only in our *actions*, not our *inactions*.

MOTIVATING THE JOURNEY

What the apathetic child is missing is the journey of life, learning and growing in a world of action and challenge. Children learn that a career decision is not a clear, linear event, that it is crazy and frustrating. They learn that we find our interests and skills and values by testing and trying and failing, that we look for the vocation of best fit, and often we find that society has too much or too little to challenge us. Such discoveries can be frightening and disillusioning. There are as many bullies and vandals in corporations as there are in schoolyards.

In the same way that an autistic person's perceptions can become overloaded with stimulation, at times your child's exploration of careers and self and the world of work will overload his perceptions. At those times, his powers of concentration will focus his attention on limited goals: the one replaces the many. Autistic people often use echolalia, the repetition of phrases said by another person, as a mechanism to prevent neurological flooding in a mind already saturated by stimuli. Focusing on one task can do the same; it gives the mind a rest yet keeps it on the road of progress.

The parent as Motivator needs to remember that there are times when helping children with career decision making has all the indignities and awkwardness of changing places in a canoe. One of the core motivations for participation in career decision making is that making decisions is what life is about; that setting goals and going after them is the essence of being alive. In life, we engage in tasks; we have the courage to be ourselves, to work at our own pace, to accomplish what is important to us. Part of life is the fun of collaborating with others. It is intriguing, even exciting, to define our personal authenticity. It is fulfilling to experience personal integration, the union of our inner and outer worlds in a merger, a harmony, that we engineered.

One of the joys of being a parent is that we have the advantage of standing outside the situation so we can witness the passing away of the old person and the coming of the new in our own growing child. We often cannot recognize the newness and change in ourselves because we are already there, we are living it now. But change that takes place during the career decision–making process is an event.

OVERCOMING "I CAN'T DO IT"

We have encouraged you to help your child remain open to new possibilities while being realistic about what it would take to make them happen (Gray 2000). We have suggested that narrowing down possibilities by eliminating what they do *not* want to do is an important part of the process. One role the parent as Motivator can take, however, is to question why they have decided to eliminate some options that once seemed to fit their interests, values, and work requirements. It may be that they have eliminated potentially rewarding choices because of faulty beliefs in their inability to do the tasks required (Brown & Lent 1996). Be especially attentive to girls who shy away from math- and science-related occupations, as studies show that many mathematically capable women discounted their capabilities and thereby unnecessarily limited their career options (Brown & Lent 1996; Hackett, Betz, O'Halloran, & Romac 1990; Campbell & Hackett 1986).

MOTIVATING EDUCATION

There is a story told in New England of a group of deer discussing a problem. Finally, with no resolution in sight, they hire an owl as a consultant. "We hear there is a wonderful place called the forest, filled with beauty, harmony, and delight," they say to the owl. "We would like to visit this place and enjoy all that it offers. Can you tell us the way?" The owl, being a wise consultant, knows that technical explanations are always well received. So she says, "Close your eyes. Turn clockwise, the sacred direction the planets move around the earth, until your intuition tells you to stop. Then open your eyes and you will be there." The deer cry, "We have no intuition, tell us how many times to turn." The owl answers, "Seven, this being the number of days in a week." Satisfied, the deer close their eyes, turn clockwise seven times, open their eyes, and see the forest for the first time.

Parents are often the owls of the career process. Children will arrive at a decision but not know they are there. One such fantastic place is the college decision.

The college decision is a critical point for learning decision-making skills. Your child should look at all the facets of the college experience: faculty, extracurricular opportunities, postgraduate jobs and careers, size and composition of the undergraduates, location, and whatever else she deems to be important.

EVALUATING FACULTY

In evaluating faculty, there are several areas where you can give encouragement in helping your child form criteria for judgment.

- Are the faculty at this college or university rewarded for research or for teaching?

- Which is more important to your child?

- What is the average class size—will your child be in her senior year before she is in a classroom with fewer than one hundred other students?

- Is the bulk of the teaching done by the faculty or by graduate students?

- Are faculty members accessible outside of class?

For instance, one student was shocked to learn, after he entered college in a town about sixty miles from a major city, that many of the faculty members commuted, often from great distances. Although he could never get an accurate figure (this was not a statistic the college wanted collected), it appeared that about one-third of the faculty were actually in town only to meet their classes. There was little opportunity for collegiality; the professors were seldom there outside of class and very limited office hours.

CONSIDERING COURSE ACCESSIBILITY

Another faculty issue to warn your child about is the competition to get into certain courses. Some high schools do not have many elective courses and those that exist rarely exclude interested students. However, college is very different. Most of the curriculum is elective, but popular courses are often open only to majors or to seniors. Your child is well-advised to ask pointed questions about course registration. Most colleges do not like to collect and publish course enrollment data relative to course preference, but a sad reality is that some courses are almost impossible to enroll in. If your child has identified several courses from the catalog that she would like to take, just as an experiment she might ask how many students are permitted to enroll and how many students are usually turned away. One student found to her horror that most of the courses she wanted to take allowed about 25 to 30 in each course out of 100 to 125 students who wanted to take the course. Getting into college is often not nearly as competitive as getting the class schedule you want.

EVALUATING CURRICULUM AND EXTRACURRICULAR ACTIVITIES

Your child is also well-advised to look at the structure of the undergraduate curriculum. What are the required courses? Is there any core curriculum requirement designed to ensure some basic competence in communications, mathematics, computer use, scientific reasoning?

An important part of any college decision is developing criteria for evaluating extracurricular activities. As Motivator, you help your child to formulate and ask questions. For instance, if his interest is in journalism and he has a desire to work on the college newspaper or radio station, find out if that is a realistic possibility. A university with a journalism school often will exclude students with other majors—for instance, history or English—from working on the campus media to keep those jobs open for journalism or communications majors.

If your daughter wants to play varsity women's basketball, help her think about how that goal will affect her school choice. If she is injured and cannot play out her full four years, is this a college she will otherwise enjoy? If she is not courted by the coach in the sport she wants, will she have any real hopes of getting play time as a walk-on? If she wants to get involved with the college theater, again find out if only drama majors are permitted to try out for major roles.

These hidden limitations can create a crisis that can be avoided with a little research. One of the key objectives in college and career decision making is doing the research necessary to make sure there are no unpleasant surprises.

EVALUATING COLLEGE CAREER SERVICES

Postgraduate career opportunities can be evaluated in reports of the career services office or any other value-added studies done by the college. These reports should be available to your child prior to admission so he can see in surveys of the graduating seniors how many went on to employment in certain career areas and how many went on to graduate school. If these surveys are either incomplete or not undertaken or simply not available to the public, that raises a serious question about the college's commitment to marketing its graduates with the same zeal it markets itself.

Your child can also ask, "How large is the admissions staff, and how large is the career planning and placement staff?" The staffing of the career center is a critical factor, and if the career center staff is less than half the size of the admissions staff, there is a problem in the priorities of that college: it is willing to sell you its services but it is unwilling to help market its own product—your child's collegiate experience. College-level career counseling offices should have one full-time professional for every 250 seniors. Other considerations regarding career counseling services are listed in Chart 9.

MAKING A DECISION

Help your child understand that what she wants is the engine force of the decision process. If she thinks she would do better in a large university environment, value that. If she wants to live at home while attending school, talk about the pros and cons. If she wants a small-school environment with high faculty interaction, talk about that.

The college decision is a critical opportunity to learn decision–making skills because the arbitration between external limitations—finances, high school grades, test scores—and internal desires is clear. Your child can use this opportunity to learn how to ask questions, gather information, consult with different experts, place relative value on different characteristics of the college experience. Your child can also learn not to rely on the glossy view books often prepared by advertising

CHART 9	*Other questions you can suggest to your child to help research the career services function at any college:*

- Is the career office online with twenty-four-hour student access?

QUESTIONS

- Does it have a home page or other services accessible to employers on the Internet?

TO ASK ABOUT

- Does the career office make student résumés available to potential employers via the Internet and/or in printed form?

COLLEGE CAREER

SERVICES

- How many employers and what kinds of employers come to recruit on campus? Is there an alumni network your child can use?

- How many alumni are in the network?

- Is there any limit on the individual career counseling time available to your child at no charge? During the autumn semester, what is the average waiting period for an appointment with a career counselor? Do seniors get preference over undergraduates in seeing a career counselor?

- Does the career office offer the *Strong Interest Inventory* and *Myers-Briggs Type Indicator* instruments?

- What kinds of instruction are offered in résumé preparation and interviewing skills? Are students offered the opportunity at no charge for a videotaped mock interview with individual critique by a professional staff member?

- What services are offered by the career counseling professional staff, and what services are offered by students acting as peer counselors and advisors?

agencies, which are a glamorous come-on with very little hard data for decision making. The complexity of decisions, the number of variables one must consider, really comes alive in your child's understanding of the decision-making process. As Motivator, you help push the number of variables being considered and keep the process going even if your child says, "You decide for me!"

MOTIVATING EMPLOYMENT

Being human means resolving, on a daily basis, the paradox of independence and community, isolation and togetherness. We are autonomous in striving for some understanding of our work, our vocation, but we may only find that work in a social context.

We have to say yes to some commitment, to some decision, in order to find ourselves within a social context for growth. Part of the wisdom of working is learning that challenges and goals organize our life. When we look back at periods of peak challenge and peak output, we usually see happy days. If we shut down our lives in lethargy and indifference, we have a formula for misery.

We have a conscience and volition and discipline and self-awareness, and employment gives us a chance to mobilize those assets. Of course, it is hard to get going, to set up one's own budget and take responsibility for all the necessary tasks of maintaining oneself—shopping, cleaning, cooking. Your child builds a work ethic as she learns that she can cruise on her aptitudes and your wallet for only so long, and then patience, practice, and commitment take over in determining who will be successful. But learning to manage time, money, credit, and her own emotional capital is hard. It often seems easier to live at home on the family payroll than to face the lessons of independence. Motivating self-reliance and self-sufficiency is the key to motivating employment. In doing that, it is helpful to take a task-oriented approach.

The number of personal bankruptcies has been climbing steadily over the last decade. Young people often get into financial difficulty managing the temptations offered by credit cards and automobile loans. Although some high schools offer a course on personal management—covering such basics as how to open a checking or savings account, how to rent an apartment, how to plan a budget—it usually falls to parents to help introduce basic financial management skills.

You need to explain to your child that he is spending his life in exchange for money and for other rewards as well — skill development, enjoyment, social recognition. Money is the core of what he receives for the days of his life. That exchange must be faced squarely. If he spends more money than he has or will receive in the short term, he will have to pay it back by mortgaging how he spends his time in the future. Money is too often an abstract concept. It appears and disappears with equal mystery. Your child needs to see that he exchanges his time and his freedom for money and that money is therefore dear. Helping your child make that connection is a big step toward vocational maturity.

How much money is enough? For a lot of new entrants to the employment world, too much is never enough. Helping your child think through such money-related decisions as an automobile purchase is an instructive lesson in how she is thinking about possessions. Children, like adults, see possessions as making a statement about who they are. "What kind of statement are you trying to make about yourself?" is a good question, and one you should ask your child about any major financial decision. Learning what we consider essential, and why, is part of growing vocationally.

If you have a healthy sense of irony, another major forum in motivating employment is talking about retirement. It is simply the case that the careers of most persons in the twenty-first century will include a period of reduced income near the end. With age discrimination happening anytime over age forty and being virtually universal over age fifty, the period of time during which we can expect diminished income is getting longer. This longer period of unemployment or underemployment may be something your child has already observed in your career. If not, it will be something he observes and needs to plan for fairly quickly in his own career. Here you can help with basic financial planning — how to save, how to select financial instruments, how to think about the future value of money. Most personal financial management is easier than your child assumes it will be from his position outside the mysteries of money.

Another area of concern in motivating employment is helping your child understand the unwritten rules of a corporate culture. Decoding the success rules in any company is one of the tasks of the first six months on the job. A related skill is learning how not to choose sides in office battles. New employees should take a moment to size up their battles before becoming one of the combatants. A lot of corporations hire aggressive, combative people who, failing to do battle with the real competition, start the rivalries and turf battles found in most large organizations. These battles are not productive. They do not encourage cooperation, teamwork, or heightened morale, nor do they produce increased competence or accelerated learning. Helping your child with some of your own street smarts might keep her out of battles that are not really hers to fight and are not encouraged by top management.

Motivating employment is about teaching your child to provide creative solutions quickly and effectively in the context of the workplace. Help your child understand key organizational goals: improved return on investment, reduced costs, streamlined systems, shortened business cycles, sustained competitive advantage.

MOTIVATING A JOB HUNT

Endurance is the critical element of success in job hunting. As Napoleon said, "The first virtue in a soldier is endurance of fatigue; courage is only secondary." The job hunter and the soldier have a lot in common. Concentration of attention and intention keeps us in touch with our humanity. The purpose of going through all the stages of the career decision–making process is to keep us from detaching from our own future. That purpose requires our resolve because the same entropic forces of degeneration and dispersion at work on our physical bodies in the aging process are working on our careers and the human organizations in which those careers take place. It is only our human effort that opposes the atrophy and nihilism that seem to be basic ingredients of life.

The major objective in every job hunt is to build a critical mass of visibility in the labor market. Again and again it has been our experience that job hunters will search without a response until suddenly the critical mass is reached and three offers appear. The challenge is to stick with working, looking at job postings either at employers' personnel offices or at sites on the Web or other online career sites, sending out large mailings of résumés, reading the want ads, visiting the state employment services, or embarking on the myriad other activities demanded by a successful job hunt. Here parental motivation is often best enacted by the words, "What can I do to help?" Remember (and keep reminding your son or daughter) what you have been practicing all along: look for opportunities to put his or her skills, interests, and values to work. Find opportunities, create them, don't wait for them to come to you. Read *What Color Is Your Parachute?* (Bolles 2003) to understand all the alternatives to traditional job search techniques. Develop relationships. Find places that would be great to work and ask for an informational interview. Even if there are no opportunities there at the moment, maybe someone in their network has one or you will have at least set the stage for a future opportunity. Use the Yellow Pages and online tools as much as or more than newspaper ads. A quick glance at the Sunday paper does not a job search make.

THE RÉSUMÉ

Job hunting is a lot like flying a small plane. We have to work hard to get up to our full altitude, but then we can really soar. The take-off point is the résumé. Résumés are pieces of our life history imprinted with our name and telephone number—how we can be contacted. In the age of computer scanners, electronic résumés placed with online services get scanned for content: Does this résumé contain at least 75 percent of the key descriptors (nouns and verbs, but give the edge to nouns) the employer is looking for? Many books offer advice on résumé preparation. Professional résumé preparation costs between $100 and $350 per résumé.

It is crucial to produce a document that is error free—no spelling lapses, no grammar glitches, no printing faux pas. When we asked a senior human resources person in a large corporation what help with résumés parents might give their kids, she said without hesitation, "Proofread!"

Help your child think about the skills she wants to document, keeping in mind that quantitative descriptors paint a good, concrete picture of her accomplishments. Help her think about what she has actually done, where she actually took ownership of a project.

Look for opportunities to use active verbs—create, champion, sustain, market, sell, analyze. Write each job description as if it is happening now; use present tense verbs even when the action was completed in the past. If your child attended special workshops or classes related to his career, get that information into the résumé—it demonstrates commitment and shows that he acquired a skill set and improved upon it.

Think about the concept of a toolbox filled with different skills that your child has acquired. Help her describe those skills—make a list and then see how many are described in the résumé. Often we find that only about a third of the skills someone has developed make it into the résumé; this is one of the critical areas professional résumé specialists work on. As your child should have learned in skills assessment, skills have all kinds of antecedents—hobbies, volunteer work, community service, group participation in school or college, working on the home computer, helping to manage the home. Do not differentiate between paid and volunteer employment in the résumé; if your child is asked what was paid and what was nonpaid, she can explain.

Help your child set up files for each job, again both paid and nonpaid, where she can save the job description, even the advertisement or posting she originally saw, performance evaluations or letters of recommendation, pay stubs, benefits information. This kind of personal personnel file is critical to maintain throughout your child's career. In the same way you should train her to keep all her old checkbooks, bank statements, tax returns, and supporting documentation, teach her that no one should ever leave a job without one or two letters from supervisors or colleagues or customers that help to document what she did in that job.

No one should leave a school or college without a letter about key extracurricular activities and a letter or two from favorite teachers. These can be in the form of a letter of introduction. Many times, high school and college students not going on to further study will neglect to get letters of recommendation. Five years later, the teachers or professors your child would have consulted are gone or have forgotten what needs to be said.

THE JOB INTERVIEW

Interviews are role playing with integrity. There is a limited amount of time in which to present information and impressions. Children have a hard time not being spontaneous or seeing interviews as anything other than on-the-spot improvisations. However, interviews are intentional conversations in a condensed time frame. A job interview is where you tell your story.

You can help your child by suggesting that the interview is analogous to a television infomercial. Think about all the time, thought, effort, and planning that go into a thirty-second commercial or a thirty-minute infomercial. An interview is an infomercial about your child. You can help script that event. A variety of books about interviewing can suggest questions and help shape responses.

The great help a parent can provide is persuading the child of the importance of preparation—doing mock interviews, getting a script together, looking over lists of potential questions, and thinking of answers. Talk through what important skills or experiences need to be emphasized. Books on interviewing talk about taking control of the interview. We think that *control* is not a good word for young people. It sounds as if the child needs to dominate the interviewer and be so rigidly scripted that nothing spontaneous can happen. Parental concern should be to help your child know what he wants to say about himself. Interviews are not a place to be a passive question answerer.

Your child needs to think about what he wants to communicate and how to say it. What will be his trademark? What will coax the interviewer into asking questions, getting interested, thinking of your child in the job? Controlling an interview is really about knowing what you need to find out about a job, a supervisor, and a corporate culture, and asking questions that give you that information about the work, the industry, and the company. If you leave an interview not knowing what you want to know, the interview has not worked.

An interview should be a frank exchange of information, a give-and-take. Personality, a sense of humor, a glimpse of responsive and thoughtful nature should emerge. Interviewing is practiced behavior, and one of the useful by-products of career exploration interviews is a certain comfort level in job interviewing. If your child's first interview is for a job she really wants, she is not going to appear as brave and imaginative as she would if it were her fifth interview. Help her see the value of interviewing first for some jobs she is not as excited about or having some mock interviews with your friends to break the ice.

Many naive job hunters in a very competitive marketplace think their job is only to sell themselves. They do not think they should be asking questions about the potential employer. Remind your child that he will spend 2,000 hours working there the first year and that he might want to know about the place before making that kind of commitment. In an age when temping or an internship is often the way to a job, he will have more insider knowledge of what the place of employment is like. If he does not have that firsthand experience, he should think about what he wants to know about the work, his colleagues, the future, the compensation, the physical environment in which the work will take place.

Will it be a shock to work forty hours a week in a room with no windows and no direct source of fresh air? Does she want a smoke-free environment? Where do people go to eat lunch? Does she get her own cubicle, or does she sit at a desk in an open room with four or five or fifty other people? Does it matter to her? Is health and dental insurance offered? How much does she pay toward insurance, and how much is paid by the employer? What kind of retirement benefits are offered? Help her to understand how important it is to participate in optional retirement programs. If she has investment options in the retirement plan, which kind of program does she want?

MOTIVATING EARLY CAREER SUCCESS

Parent as Motivator is a tribute to the Vince Lombardi axiom that fatigue makes cowards of us all. By the time we see our child launched into early career successes, we ourselves may want to sit down for a rest. The best is yet to be for both parents and children. Motivation 101 teaches us that we seek with the greatest energy and zeal the things of which we were deprived, or think that we were deprived, in childhood. Next to those things, we search for those experiences that consistently won us rewards in childhood.

Your child's career is rolling along. He understands the advantages and disadvantages of certain behaviors before he undertakes them. He knows that he cannot be given knowledge, he can only be stimulated to learn for himself. His goals are clear. He cherishes feedback and knows how to use it. He can concentrate his attention on the task at hand. He trusts himself enough to put down his shield of defenses and become unself-consciously involved in what he needs to do. He is choosing intrinsically rewarding experiences, volunteering for new assignments so he can learn new skills. In short, he is a success. At the peak of his productivity he gets downsized out of a job and asks you, with the same look he had when he was two, "Why?" On that day, you know that you are loved because he looks to you for light. Of course, there is no answer. Explaining the inexplicable is just part of the daily fare of being a parent. Washington Irving said that "great minds have purposes while others have wishes." Help him back to his basic purposes in life. In the face of adversity, we revisit our basic goals and skills and interests for renewal and strength. And then we start again.

BUILDING COMMITMENTS

This is the time to ask your child, What are you committed to? What goals do you have for your life? What do you want to be your trademark, the contribution people remember? Those focused desires, conscious or unconscious, will direct the aspects of her life that are under her control. They also help her regain some command of those aspects of her life that are under external control, such as work when it is taken away. It is perhaps the best test of character that your child has learned where she begins and where she ends, what she will accept and what she will reject. Careers are made in the exercise of principled judgments.

It is during those periods of unemployment that children rely the most on the lessons you as parent have taught. During unemployment, if the mind has nothing to do, no focus of attention, it will gravitate to the personal problem that is most disturbing and painful. Just when your child needs to focus on problem solving, she will start thinking obsessively about a problem that has nothing to do with getting a job. Apparently this reaction is due to a residue of primordial evolution: in a crisis, we unconsciously flash back to a pale-olithic savanna and scan the horizon for threats. Of course, the saber-toothed tiger of unemployment is right in front of us, but instead of responding directly to that beast, we cannot stop looking for the next attack. The mind will focus on real or imaginary pain or on whatever negative feelings it can find. Parents can help overcome this natural negativity by moving the focus of attention and action to the many real objectives that need elbow grease if your child is to find a new job.

CAREER TRANSITIONS

Career development scholars are at the edge of developing a theory of cognitive readiness for career transitions. That theory, when it is fully understood, will probably be based on our growth in ability to make meaning, to create comprehension of the context in which career changes are taking place. Our human meaning-making function will probably be seen as rooted in the ability to construct significance from autobiographical memory, to understand what events mean to us, in order to determine our own unique defining factors.

Our ability to make meaning usually grows as we progressively differentiate ourselves from our world in order to establish our own distinct identity. Having established that unique voice, or identity, or sense of self, we then have to work at reintegrating ourselves through a network of commitments, values, principles. We have to be individuals before we can authentically join a community, yet paradoxically we need community to support us as we grow into our individuality.

Children often try to respond to a cacophony of voices giving direction and advice. In cases such as Babette's, which we discussed earlier, those voices are taking over the child's identity. If the child is seeking only to meet the demands of others, her own creativity and self-expression will not have the appropriate arena in which to develop.

The self-assertiveness found in unemployment transitions is fertile ground for growth. As Motivator, your role is to help your child focus on the growth potential in the situation.

In a sense, the loss of employment casts the child out into a world that he must construct for himself. The external structure of job expectations and organizational cues has been ripped away by unemployment and he must have some internal mechanisms, a strength of character or self-esteem, that sustain him. The codependencies with you or with his employer are exposed when the employment pact is broken and he has lost his source of direction. The quid pro quo "You do what I tell you to do and I will give you a job" stifled his growth of a sense of self as career-maker, and when that authority is withdrawn he is lost. The self-assertiveness found in unemployment transitions is fertile ground for growth. As Motivator, your role is to help your child focus on the growth potential in the situation. That help is largely in the form of returning to the career decision–making process and getting back to work.

Children develop a vision of their own careers. That vision operates the way a hypothesis operates in guiding a scientific experiment. The vision serves as a basis for a self-authored career. As Motivator, getting to the vision of self-authored career path is an objective to keep in mind always. In a period of unemployment, the important questions your child should ask herself are, Where am I going? Which jobs are my best forms of self-expression?

These questions and exercises help you understand what defining pressures you have placed, intentionally or unintentionally, on the child. Those pressures, from you or from significant others, create a decision-making predicament. The child's long-term success as a worker and as an adult is based on her growing capacity to construct a meaningful future. We have found that the career decision–making process described in this book provides parents with caring and yet challenging methodology.

In a period of unemployment, there are opportunities for transformation and for transition. Transformation takes place when the child returns to those basic defining goals, values,

QUESTIONS TO ASK YOUR CHILD

THE PARENT AS MOTIVATOR

- You seemed excited when learning about that career field. What especially interested you?

- You have learned a lot about yourself through this process. How can we keep the momentum going?

- You seem stuck at this point. What might be causing that, and how can you move forward?

- How do you know that this move is right for you?

- What will taking this job cost you?

- What do you gain if you take this job?

- Forget about trying to please everyone; how does this job please you?

- Describe what you think our parental expectations are.

- Describe what your own expectations are.

and interests to see how he is changing. Transition is moving from one job opportunity to another or from one career field to another. In both transformational and transitional activities, your child is in charge of his career. That self-awareness of personal authority for career direction is critical at this stage of growth. You, as Motivator, try to keep returning him to that core awareness. As comfortable as it might feel to have someone else in charge of his career, he is nevertheless in charge; he determines if his interests are present or absent in any particular opportunity.

The parent's role always boils down to love: giving time, attention, care, concern; asking clarifying questions; connecting your child with herself; providing motivation for clear unequivocal behavior; helping her to make happen what needs to happen; challenging when necessary to close the gap between goals and performance; helping to downscale goals when that is necessary.

PRISCILLA'S STORY

Priscilla was not a good student. The message she got from school was that she was below average. Her parents heard from teachers that Priscilla had low motivation and showed signs of laziness. In high school, she was more interested in boys, her hair, clothes, and makeup than in homework. The book she studied most closely was the driver's manual needed to pass her state driver's license exam. Priscilla completed high school but drifted from job to job. Her habits in school carried over to the workplace, and she found herself fired twice for a "performance deficit." Her managers complained she was chronically late for work and continually dodged responsibility. She drifted in and out of substance abuse, alcohol being her drug of choice.

Early on, Priscilla's parents had decided not to push their ideas or concerns but simply to let Priscilla live her own life. Their attitude changed when Priscilla moved home after the second job loss. Her job hunting was not going well and her apathy grew to the point where she had gone six weeks without an interview. Priscilla's father was forced into an early retirement when his company downsized him out of a job at age fifty-five and no one wanted to hire him. Her mother was trying to get a home-based business off the ground, so money was very tight. Her parents resented Priscilla's dependency but she apparently didn't care.

Priscilla's mother, Virginia, had taken a time-management seminar as part of her own preparations for running a home-based business. With these goal-setting skills fresh in her mind, Virginia sat down with Priscilla and explained that continuing to live at home while not working was not one of Priscilla's options. Virginia helped Priscilla set a goal of five job interviews in the coming week. They looked at the help-wanted adver-tisements in the Sunday newspaper. They got on the Internet and looked at the Job Web (www.job-web.org) and other similar sites with job listings. They found that local companies with Web sites usually have a link from the home page to listings of job openings in that company.

The local YWCA sponsored a series of workshops on job-hunting skills, which Virginia attended with Priscilla. Virginia had gotten herself a membership in a local health and fitness club, which allowed her to bring Priscilla once a week for a workout. Priscilla loved the club, and the goal of getting her own membership became a driving force motivating her job hunt.

Within eight weeks, Priscilla had gotten a job. A few months later, she told her mother that she had been able to get started because Virginia had challenged her to take charge of her own life and then had given her the resources she needed—the biggest resource being her love.

KEY ACTIONS

THE PARENT AS MOTIVATOR

- Help your child to overcome nonchalance that may be simply disguising a fear of failure.

- Help your child understand the combination of liberty and necessity that governs most of our lives.

- Provide support in a family setting.

- Remember that one of the core motivations for participation in career decision making is that making decisions is what life is about.

- Help to increase the number of variables being considered.

- Keep the decision-making process going even when your child says, "You decide for me!"

- Help your child understand that endurance is the critical element of success in job hunting.

- In times of unemployment, help your child focus on the growth potential in that situation.

CAREER PLANNING AS

YOUR CHILD GROWS

N PART ONE, we looked at career planning from a generic "your child" perspective. Your own career satisfaction, and your experience with parental influences in your career, were explored. We suggested that you be aware of the balance between underinvolvement and overinvolvement in your children's career decisions.

In Part Two, we presented a career decision–making model, and we discussed the roles you play during each step in that process. In Part Three, we look at career planning as it plays out during three age ranges: childhood, adolescence, and young adulthood. We hesitate to define specific ages because of bias against stage theories that imply that all twelve-year-olds experience the same phenomena and should be engaging in identical activities. In fact, we have found wide variations in the behavior and needs of twelve-, sixteen-, and twenty-five-year-olds. Categorizing by wide age ranges as we have may suggest a level of sameness, which is unintended. Obviously no two twelve-year-olds are exactly alike—in genetics, appearance, aspirations, or developmental needs.

With these caveats, we do believe there is value in looking at career planning from a developmental stage perspective. We offer this overview of developmental tasks at various stages to frame various career activities for each stage. You decide which discussions best describe your child's current experience and behavior, regardless of his or her specific age. If you have more than one child, you will want to read through the rest of this book with each child in mind.

Beyond these considerations, we urge you to look at each child as a unique individual—with unique interests, skills, values, personality, and aspirations. A successful strategy for dealing with one child does not necessarily mean success working with another. Even if they are in the same developmental stage, they may have very different needs and desires and may reveal entirely different personalities. Ask any multiple-birth parent how alike and different their children are. Though siblings play an important role in modeling, influencing, and mentoring one another, each child's career decision making is a unique challenge and responsibility. Just as you can love your children equally but are able to build unique relationships with each one, so too you can provide different but equal levels of career support.

In this part of the book, we describe each major category from the perspective of

- The major developmental tasks within each stage

- Likely career planning tasks

- Helpful parental interventions

- Suggestions about what not to do

We assign the labels *early* and *later* to each age category, (e.g., early childhood, later childhood). These labels may or may not correspond to other stage-related theories of human development. As you have no doubt discovered in other aspects of parenting, all children do not and need not correspond to average age estimates.

8

APPROPRIATE INTRODUCTIONS AT CHILDHOOD

HILDHOOD ENCOMPASSES a wide range of activities, transitions, and accomplishments. It is marked by a combination of dependence and autonomy seeking, by endearing connections with and rebellious independence from adults. We have defined early childhood as infancy through preschool years (birth to age six) and later childhood as grade school years (ages six to twelve).

Though too early for most of the formal career planning tasks such as assessments and job search activities, childhood sets an important foundation for later years. Children's sense of wonder can be encouraged to help them identify myriad possibilities for their future. Emotional intelligence and confidence, necessary for success in any field, can be developed.

A sense of responsibility and work ethic can be fostered through early academic and odd-job responsibilities. Most important, parents provide role models and messages about work to their children in their earliest years that will last and impact them for a lifetime.

EARLY CHILDHOOD: BIRTH TO AGE SIX

DEVELOPMENTAL TASKS

One of the key developmental tasks in early childhood, as described by classic developmental theorist Erik Erikson, is the establishment of trust in significant other people, particularly parents. This bond will continue to develop throughout the child's and the parents' lifetimes. According to Erikson (1968), the degree to which children believe their parents can be counted on to be there for them throughout their lifetimes is contingent on their perceptions of having had their early needs met as dependent infants. As they explore their new world, they vacillate between testing limits and maintaining connection with the person whose primary responsibility is to take care of them.

The latter part of early childhood is marked by an increasing confidence that they can do things for themselves and by the ensuing struggle for autonomy and independence. Through preschool and early school activities, they enter social worlds and structured environments that extend beyond their immediate extended families. Peter Favaro (1995) noted that this period extends the stresses of learning to regulate oneself physically to include "increased social demands such as learning to share, taking turns, and giving up an object that belongs to someone else. All of these changes together result in your child's life being both exciting and tumultuous. In many ways, it is a period of greater self-definition and interdependence than adolescence is."

BADMINTON, ANYONE?

Diana remembers standing on top of the picnic table singing into the handle of a badminton racket. Later she would use the "microphone" to discuss preschool world affairs with Teddy the Bear on her imaginary talk show. Therein lay the foundations for adult public performances as a corporate trainer and for investigative skills to lead academic research.

Your child the upcoming mechanical engineer, on the other hand, has the racket pulled apart and reconfigured before you can catch what he or she is doing. A future professional model uses it as a mirror. Investigative types discover a magnifying glass to search for clues. Some athletes and potential fitness professionals may even use the badminton racket for its intended purpose as a sporting instrument.

CAREER PLANNING TASKS

As we developed these chapters of the book, we asked numerous career planning and child development professionals their opinions about when career planning activities should begin. We got a variety of answers, ranging from concerns about pushing children to grow up too fast to getting as early a start as possible. It was perhaps during these discussions that we realized how important it is to expand the definition of career planning beyond the perception of sitting down and formally assessing one's future vocation. Career planning encompasses all activities that help people become aware of their interests, abilities, values, and options.

Expressed interests are those that are discovered and articulated in multiple natural and unstructured ways. One child can sit for hours playing with Legos while another pushes them aside. One may show a propensity for outdoor adventurous events, while another enjoys quiet time inside drawing pictures and reading books. These expressed interests can be observed without any type of formal assessment process. Assessed interests are those likes and dislikes that are discovered through formal tools such as the *Murphy-*

Meisgeier Type Indicator for Children assessment (the childhood version of the *Myers-Briggs Type Indicator* personality inventory).

Early childhood is one of the richest times to discover, observe, and nurture career interests and perceptions. Eavesdrop on a pair of four-year-olds next time they are playing school, store, or doctor. Childhood is a period of intense imagination, what career theorist Eli Ginzberg calls the "fantasy stage." Children act out their career fantasies through the roles they design for themselves in play scenarios and in the kinds of play activities they choose to pursue. The major career planning tasks of early childhood are discovering and expressing interests and skills through imagination, play, and pretending (Montross and Shinkman, 1992).

PARENTAL INVOLVEMENT

Besides all the other critical roles you play in your child's early years, you can foster their career planning success in several ways. Foremost in those early childhood days is the foundation of trust that Erikson described, which will set the stage for the relationship you will need to positively influence your children throughout their lifetimes. If they believe you are trustworthy, caring, and there for them, then they will later in life accept your sincerity in wanting to help them discover what's best for them from a vocational standpoint. They need to know throughout their preadult lifetimes that there are adults on whom they can count for their basic and support needs. These beliefs will carry into adulthood, where a sense of trust may mean the difference between positive and negative mental health.

It is important that you continuously foster, not discourage, your children's sense of adventure and imagination. In an earlier example, Jill's parents, embarrassed by her clamoring for attention, devalued and squashed her potential for public performance. Give your children a chance to express and explore their interests. Talk about their perceptions of how the world operates as you observe their play, especially if they have picked up stereotypes such as boys always play the doctor and girls always play the nurse. Intervene with an interested discussion if you overhear statements such as "girls can't be a fireman" or "brothers have to play the bad guy." Do not allow other adults to inflict those biases or limitations on your child. Consistently reinforce multiple and varied options.

Another vital role you can play during the early stages of your child's natural career exploration process is one that follows throughout his or her life: the parent as the most influential role model. During our career planning workshops with adults, we ask them to remember what they wanted to be when they grew up. Most often their replies point to an occupation related to a role model in their life, usually related to what Mom or Dad did for a living. You are your child's first example of what it means to operate in the world.

Modeling career happiness and success (defined as satisfaction and fit with your skills and interests) matters more than perhaps anything else you can do. Especially during these early years, children watch your every move, pay attention to your reactions, and emulate your lifestyle. If you want to grumble about how unfair your manager is being, do so after the kids are in bed. If you have anxiety about making the next mortgage payment, discuss it with your adult partner, not in front of your children. If you get a promotion or have had a particularly good day at work, visibly celebrate your success.

In addition to acting as a role model yourself, introduce your children to people in a wide variety of occupations, including women and men in nontraditional roles. Invite them on field trips to the fire station or city hall. Discuss people's occupations as you meet them in malls, doctor's offices, and banks. When your children are searching for games to play, suggest pretending to be occupational characters you have met together during the past week. Note their language and activities during the pretending and discuss their perceptions with them.

CHART 10	**Developmental tasks** ■ Establish trust with significant others, parents ■ Develop confidence in ability to do things for themselves
	Career planning tasks ■ Foster imagination, play, fantasy roles
EARLY CHILDHOOD: BIRTH TO AGE SIX	**Parental involvement** ■ Discuss and encourage multiple options ■ Use self as strong role model ■ Introduce child to diverse role models
	What not to do ■ Do not discourage imaginative thinking ■ Do not perpetuate stereotypes and limitations ■ Do not yet administer formal career assessment "testing"

WHAT NOT TO DO

The worst thing parents can do when their child is at this age is to discourage the creativity of the youngster's imaginings. It is not silly for a five-year-old to want to be an astronaut, or a television star, or the president of the United States. Although later these aspirations may feel out of reach, early dreams point to interests and values. They provide the opportunity for discussion about what is important to your child and how he or she currently understands the world. This is not a good time to discuss why your child should have aspirations higher than driving the local garbage truck, though you certainly may have bigger dreams for him or her. Your child may be indicating a propensity for "realistic" kinds of work, for working with his or her hands, for mechanical abilities. It's more appropriate to say, "That might be interesting work. Why would you want to do that?" than "I'm sure you can find something a little more glamorous to do with your life."

We and the experts we consulted all agreed that it is probably too early to begin any type of formal assessments of career interests beyond those already discussed. The danger in introducing perceived "tests" is that people (children and parents) begin to limit and narrow the child's options based on "what the test said they should be." We watch carefully that our adult clients understand that instrumentation is only a perspective from which to understand their aspirations, not a pat and inflexible "answer." Children provide enough rich data on their own without administering formal processes at this point. Let them play and have fun, and enjoy observing as their personalities and interests emerge.

LATER CHILDHOOD: AGES SIX TO TWELVE

DEVELOPMENTAL TASKS

Later childhood years are industrious ones for most children. They begin to operate within the formal educational structure and are held responsible for homework, spelling tests, and showing up to class on time. They are now influenced by a wider circle of role models, primarily teachers and other educational figures (such as principals, guidance counselors, school office personnel, etc.). They participate in projects and peer activities, such as organized sports, on a regular basis. They are able to concentrate longer and attend to their activities in a more focused and deliberate way. They learn to read and they begin to establish the ability to think abstractly. They develop strong same-sex friendships and establish new kinds of relationships with parents and family members. The impending onset of puberty brings about physical and hormonal changes that affect the child's self-image.

CAREER PLANNING TASKS

Perhaps the most pertinent, positive, and frightening aspect of career planning during later childhood is that children accept and explore the meaning of their existence in the larger world outside the home. They take on the task of learning skills that will equip them for that expanded identity.

KATY'S STORY

Katy was a quiet girl and had what she would later discover was called an introverted personality. She preferred individual activities such as reading and drawing to competitive physical sports. Katy's first response to the question "What do you want to be when you grow up?" was a teacher, though she would quickly add that she wouldn't like standing in front of the room. She didn't even like reading aloud in class! As an adult, Katy clearly recalls conversations with her mother that helped shape her thinking about her future. She remembered Mom asking her why she wanted to teach (to help other children, she said; to share her knowledge; to have the authority to grade the papers).

They brainstormed how she might fulfill her interest in teaching without being the center of attention. She could be the teacher's aide, working with kids individually to help them understand the lessons the teacher had taught. She could be the principal, a job that she perceived as sitting in your office waiting for children to come to see you. She could join a school that did not have very many kids in each class. She could be a guidance counselor.

Then they talked about how, if she decided that she still wanted to teach, she could develop the skills and confidence to get up in front of the room and do it. One way to start, Mom suggested, might be to participate in school plays, which Katy did and enjoyed for many years. Maybe the teacher would let her help pass out homework assignments. With her mother's help and encouragement, she spoke with all her teachers and created a list of where they had gone to school, how they had decided to become teachers, and how they had gotten over the stage fright of standing in the front of the room. To her surprise, more than half of the teachers she talked with shared her introverted personality!

Finally they talked about ways other than teaching that a person can share her knowledge and help people, and came up with a long list of occupations that Katy hadn't considered, such as social worker or probation officer. She could be a professor or researcher. Instead of reading the schoolbooks aloud, she could write them. During Katy's later middle school years, she shifted her aspirations in that direction and decided that she would become a writer. They went through similar discussions about what that might mean (newspaper journalist, poet, lyricist, playwright, nonfiction author).

After graduating from a local community college, Katy found herself in a production position at her state's largest employer, a job she didn't care for but that she did to earn money to live on her own. She saw no connection between her job and career aspirations until she interviewed for a corporate training position, in which many of her interests seemed to come together. The job gave her responsibilities for writing company training manuals and for career counseling employees. This and subsequent human resource positions helped her develop public speaking and writing skills. Katy eventually started her own career counseling practice and presents evening lectures based on her publications and experiences. She attributes her ambition and success to early encouragement and assistance she got from her family and mentors, which took a dream of helping others and opened up possibilities of how to make it happen. Had Mom said, "You're too shy to be a teacher," her dreams might have ended there.

Erikson (1968) called this the *inferiority* or *industry* stage. Later childhood can be a stressful time similar to the experience many parents and adults feel on the job, as middle and junior high school academic and social demands become your child's career. Older children are told they must work hard to succeed at future activities such as those they will encounter in high school. They increasingly become aware of their ability to influence what happens to them.

Eli Ginzberg (1979) identified the period before age eleven as the "fantasy choice" period, where "children believe they can become whatever they want to become." Donald Super (Montross & Shinkman 1992) identified birth to age twelve as the "growth" period, during which occupations are not of central concern, but curiosity and role models lead children to explore their possibilities. This, you may say, is the age of dreams. Let them dream, help them dream. Help them find new images on which to build their imaginations.

PARENTAL INVOLVEMENT

You may feel sad and frightened to watch your child venture off to the influences of the wider society and wonder about the extent to which your own influence will wane. Yet research continues to indicate that despite the increasing role of education and peers during later childhood and adolescence, parents are still considered the most influential and important figures in their children's lives (White, 1994). Children increasingly place importance on separating the home, school, and social aspects of their lives, but they thrive on their parents' affection nonetheless.

By later childhood, some patterns of career interest may be emerging. If possible, help your child link short-term odd jobs to areas of interest. For example, if your daughter or son expresses interest in a trade such as carpentry, then odd jobs at the local lumber store might be a good fit. If he or she seems to be leaning toward an academic career such as college teaching, you may want to take your child to night

CHART 11

In addition to maintaining your position as a positive role model and consistently encouraging diverse occupational alternatives, there are some practical steps you can take during your children's later childhood to foster a sense of responsibility, positive self-concept, and understanding of the world of work:

BUILDING RESPONSIBILITY

- Help your children succeed at their first "career" by helping them with homework and school projects. (This does not mean doing their work for them! Help develop study habits and thinking skills.)

- Consistently give them encouragement and feedback on accomplishments and effort.

- Be sensitive to sibling teasing and negative comments that may become more significant to your preteen than you can understand.

- Introduce earned income and money management skills, as long as they do not interfere with their primary school career.

- Establish routine chores for which they take responsibility. Encourage them to find odd jobs such as painting, paper routes, childcare, etc., that earn them a salary.

- Begin providing an allowance, and help them open a savings account. Challenge them to set financial goals. Saving up for a new bike goes a long way toward understanding investment and budgeting concepts as well as working toward a long-term objective.

school with you or see if the local library needs any assistance. If your child expresses interest in health care, he or she may want to take over some responsibilities such as visiting elders in a nursing home. Encourage community and volunteer service as well as paid work by positioning them as free learning opportunities.

If no consistent interests seem to be evolving by age twelve, you can consider introducing a formal skills assessment tool, but it is still early and this could just as easily wait until early adolescence. Continue supportive yet nonaggressive discussions about what interests your child and provide opportunities to explore those interests. Constantly encourage exploration through

CHART 12	**Developmental tasks**
	▪ Participate in formal education, projects, peer activities
	▪ Form a wider circle of role models, strong same-sex friendships
	▪ Develop ability to concentrate longer, learn to read, think abstractly
LATER CHILDHOOD: AGES SIX TO TWELVE	**Career planning tasks**
	▪ Begin to explore their possibilities
	▪ Apply themselves to schoolwork and chores
	▪ Take on demanding school and social expectations
	Parental involvement
	▪ Maintain position as positive role model and provide consistent encouragement of diverse alternatives
	▪ Help with homework and school projects
	▪ Routine chores, allowance, odd jobs, and bank accounts
	What not to do
	▪ Do not let odd jobs get in the way of academic success
	▪ Do not get discouraged when experimentation produces an apparent lack of focus and commitment

reading via frequent trips to the library and bookstore. Steps you can take to help build your child's responsibility are listed in Chart 11.

WHAT NOT TO DO

Celebrate your child's graduation into this more mature phase of childhood, and don't despair about decreasing dependence on you. Let your child know that you are always there when you are needed. Give the assistance needed with homework and study aids, but do not take on the responsibility that needs to be undertaken by the student. Establish chores and allow odd jobs, but do not let them get in the way of your child's academic success. Begin to provide a regular allowance but do not make a habit of freely handing out money that will decrease the incentive to earn it. Research suggests that it is not a good idea to tie allowance to regular chores, as it should be considered part of the responsibility of all family members to pitch in. Some specific "beyond expectations" tasks could be paid jobs that earn them extra money, but be careful that you don't instill a sense of entitlement in which they expect to be paid for everything you ask them to do (McCurrach 2003). Finally, if you begin to take your children to work with you more often (as we suggest), remember that this does not mean that they are going to follow in your footsteps—unless that's what they really want to do.

9

WHAT TO EXPECT DURING ADOLESCENCE

WE DIVIDE THIS STAGE into two segments, early adolescence (ages twelve to fourteen) and later adolescence (ages fifteen to seventeen). We call the later stages of eighteen and beyond *young adulthood*, though some books refer to the ages of eighteen to twenty-two as late adolescence. Remember, though, that these age groupings are somewhat arbitrary, and your child may experience these developmental tasks earlier or later. We provide the ages as guideposts and identifiers and suggest that you try to identify where your child is based on the description of activities, not chronological age. As a 1995 study by the Carnegie Council on Adolescent Development notes, "adolescents vary greatly in their physical development, life experiences, values, and aspirations. Even individuals of the same age differ enormously in their growth patterns, personalities, aptitudes, and coping skills."

We begin this chapter with a discussion of two overall debates about the nature of the adolescent experience, followed by a description of developmental tasks, career planning activities undertaken by youths of this stage, suggestions for potential parental interventions, and recommendations about what not to do.

THE NATURE OF ADOLESCENCE

Though debates among developmental scholars and researchers exist about stages of the entire human life span, none are as pronounced as those surrounding the developmental stage called adolescence. Foremost among these is the debate about whether teens strive for separation and autonomy or for connection and relationship. The establishment of a self-identity separate from parents and disengagement from parental control have long been identified as key tasks adolescents face. Some now challenge this focus on independence and autonomy, noting that studies that reached those conclusions were conducted almost exclusively with males. They suggest that adolescent development for girls rests on standards of connection and that the main task for an adolescent girl is to understand herself in relation to others (Jorden et al. 1991; Gilligan 1982).

Another debate is about the very nature of adolescence. For decades, the teenage years were considered a time of turmoil, in which adolescents and all who knew them endured *storm and stress*, a term introduced by Stanley Hall in 1904. It was a place of limbo, on the fringes of childhood and adulthood, not fitting into either space. Today the notion that adolescence must be a time of extreme turmoil is disputed, though it is still considered a time of transition and significant change, and the person who enters adolescence in the seventh or eighth grade is very different from the person who emerges as a high school graduate. That transition needn't be consumed by constant tumultuous conflict and anxiety, though as a parent it may sometimes seem that way.

We proceed on the assumption that there is sufficient support for both sides of the debate about the fundamental tasks of adolescence and suggest that ego identity and connection are not mutually exclusive ideas. We propose that adolescence is both a time of declaring oneself a unique individual, with needs, interests, and values exactly like no one else, and a time when relationship with others—including one's parents—is of utmost importance. We liken it to the earliest childhood bonds between parent and child, in which trust and connection were the keys to the independence of first footsteps. We also acknowledge that adolescence can be a trying and difficult age, though not necessarily more so than childhood and adulthood, and not equally so in all situations. The developmental tasks outlined below suggest some reasons why this period may seem so stressful.

EARLY ADOLESCENCE: AGES TWELVE TO FOURTEEN

DEVELOPMENTAL TASKS

Adolescent egocentrism: adolescents believe that others are as obsessed with their behavior and appearance as they are.

Adolescent researcher David Elkind (1994) suggested that much of the perceived "storm and stress" of adolescent behavior comes from the fact that "the adolescent transition is unique. It is a period of extremely rapid physical, emotional, psychological, and social growth." Elkind had earlier (1967) described a behavior that contributed to perceptions of extreme difficulty in early adolescence, a preoccupation he called *adolescent egocentrism*. "Because they believe attention is focused on them, they frequently behave as though they were performing before an assemblage of people. A good deal of adolescent boorishness, loudness, and faddish dress is probably provoked partially by a failure to differentiate between what the young person believes to be attractive and what others admire. They fail to understand why adults disapprove of the way they dress and behave."

So if you have heard yourself asking in exasperation whether your teenagers believe that the world revolves around them, the answer may be yes. They may not want to walk down the street with Mom where everyone will see, and heaven forbid you should show affection in public. Hours are spent in front of the mirror preparing for their performance before an imaginary public audience. They agonize over acne that they fear everyone will notice and hairstyles that they expect everyone to either admire or ridicule. Their egocentrism goes both ways, and they believe that others magnify both their perceived good and their perceived bad qualities.

Some theorists and parents believe that this phenomenon strikes girls harder than boys. Elkind suggests that egocentrism peaks by ages thirteen to fourteen, and by age sixteen most adolescents have developed a less idealistic and less self-centered view.

Physical changes in adolescence create just cause for many young people's attention to their self-image, and creating and maintaining a positive self-concept can be a trying challenge in a culture that promotes narrow definitions of beauty. It is widely believed that pubescent adolescents are prey to "raging hormones," with the implication that they are out of control and that little can be done to influence them. The drastic changes in secretion of sex hormones during early adolescence do have profound effects on every tissue of the body—most notably the reproductive system and the brain. These hormones produce the growth spurt, secondary sex characteristics, and feelings of sexual arousal. They also herald an increase in emotional intensity, with girls experiencing more depression and boys experiencing more aggression.

"But these changes do not mean that young adolescents are inherently difficult, contrary, or uneducatable. The effects of these changes are highly influenced by social and interpersonal factors. When such influences are positive, the biological transition goes more smoothly" (Paikoff and Brooks-Gunn 1990). Social learning researchers such as Albert Bandura (1986) have long suggested that problems attributed to adolescents are born from the society in which

> *"These changes do not mean that young adolescents are inherently difficult, contrary, or uneducatable."*
>
> Paikoff and Brooks-Gunn, 1990

they are immersed, a theory supported by a 1995 Carnegie Council report, which cited the impact of the media, the changing structure of families and work, and the influence of violence as societal factors in a young person's development.

Dualistic thinking: adolescents believe that there are two options, one way or the other, with nothing in between.

Finally, a developmental task of the early adolescent that may provoke difficult behavior is the gradual realization that everything does not have to be at one extreme or the other, a preadolescent tendency that William Perry (Belenky 1986) called *dualistic thinking*. Your child may see things as black and white with no room for gray, but this tendency eventually gives way to what Perry calls *multiplicity*, the ability to envision multiple ways of approaching problems and situations.

CAREER PLANNING TASKS

Early adolescence is the time for first part-time jobs such as paper routes, baby-sitting, and yardwork, in which your child may for the first time earn money from someone besides Mom or Dad. This is an important first step toward developing a sense of responsibility and accomplishment.

School is still a young teenager's primary career, though, and most adolescents experience an important transition from grade school or junior high school into the secondary school environment. This can be a trying time for egocentric thirteen-year-olds, who enter the first year of high school feeling the need to start anew developing the stature and confidence they grew to expect in the last years of elementary school. To them, their success in school may be measured by the development of their social standing among peers and upperclassmates.

This is not unlike the workplace experience, where job accomplishments are measured within the realm of socio-political relationships with more senior members of an organization. Parents may downplay the importance of their children's social acceptance, much as many employees dismiss the importance of workplace politics in the name of meritocracy. In both cases, social standing cannot take the

CHART 13

Your children's interests and skills will continue to evolve and become evident as they get involved with school and extracurricular activities and through the kinds of books and magazines they read, the music they listen to, and the friends with whom they share their adolescent experience.

SPOTTING INTERESTS AND SKILLS

- What did they ask for as their last birthday or holiday gifts? Are they into sports and activities that involve large groups, such as ball games, or do they prefer more solitary activities, such as biking or video games?

- Do they enjoy detailed games that require logic and forethought, such as chess, Risk, or Battleship, or do they go for games such as Pictionary™, which require creative imagination?

- Do they keep a journal or diary?

- Do they sing and dance to their favorite music?

- Do they hang out with big crowds of kids or spend most of their time with one best friend?

- Are they seen as leaders or followers?

place of hard work and school/job accomplishments—nor can it be ignored.

All these teenage activities, as well as those mentioned in Chart 13, begin to identify the skills and interests that may play a role in your child's career aspirations. Although they may not appear to be related to career planning, these leisure-time activities may begin pointing to the kinds of work that your child will or will not enjoy.

PARENTAL INVOLVEMENT

As during their childhood, you are still an important role model for your young teenage children, so continue to demonstrate the kinds of behaviors you hope to see them adopt. Perhaps the two most crucial qualities a parent must possess during his or her child's early adolescent period are patience and empathy. Remember that your child may be going through difficult physical, emotional, and social transitions, and try to recall your own experiences during this age. Though he or she may appear uninterested, stories (positive and negative) about how you handled your first days in high school or how you battled pimples and bad hair days go a long way toward showing that even though adolescence may seem difficult, one can survive it and succeed. Talk with your child about the similarities between high school and corporate hallways. Empathize with his or her laughter one day and tears the next: Don't you feel that way sometimes?

Support the desire to take on a part-time early job, and help your child understand the responsibility that goes with it. Give your children more challenging work around the house as their level of trustworthiness increases. Treat lack of responsibility seriously, and reward responsible behavior with praise and increased autonomy. Help them balance paid work with academic work, and remind them that school must remain a primary concern.

Show your children statistics that prove staying in school is important, and help them see the applications and significance of what they are learning. Remain involved in school and after-school activities. Encourage them to participate in nonschool events, and help them determine the activities that interest them, not you. Consistently praise them for their natural and acquired abilities, whatever they are. Casually mention that they are better dancers than you, or comment on their ability to always beat you at chess. This is an age when they are discovering and enhancing the natural skills and capacities that will help them succeed later in their careers.

WHAT NOT TO DO

Given their propensity to believe that all eyes are on them, refrain from making any kind of disparaging remarks about their appearance. If they're being lazy and uncooperative, comment on how that behavior is annoying you right now, but

CHART 14

EARLY

ADOLESCENCE:

AGES TWELVE

TO FOURTEEN

Developmental tasks
- Focus on self-image, egocentrism, "all eyes on me"
- Undergo physical and hormonal changes
- Develop dualistic, "one way or the other" thinking

Career planning tasks
- Take on first jobs (e.g., paper route, baby-sitting)
- Discover interests through extracurricular activity
- Experience transition to high school

Parental involvement
- Maintain position as positive role model, empathize
- Support early work experience
- Maintain active role in school activities
- Praise development of abilities and responsible behavior

What not to do
- Do not make disparaging remarks about appearance or motivation
- Do not downplay their social dilemmas and teenage concerns
- Do not do their after-school work for them

refrain at all costs from making such comments as, "You'll never amount to anything," which can have long-term damaging effects and can become a self-fulfilling prophesy. Do not coerce your children into participating in extracurricular activities in which you excelled if that's not what they are interested in doing. Encourage them to find alternative ways to spend their time. Finally, in an effort to support their first-time employment opportunities, do not do their work for them. Driving from door to door to deliver newspapers is a nice gesture during inclement weather, but it becomes your paper route rather than theirs. If you don't trust the neighborhood to which they are delivering papers, help them find an alternative.

Elizabeth Fenwick and Tony Smith (1996) offer additional suggestions:

- In all circumstances, make sure that working does not interfere with schoolwork or affect your child's health.

- Beware of employers looking to take unfair advantage of adolescents as a source of cheap labor. A teen may be willing to work for as little as half the going rate of an adult to do the same work, but you should not allow your child to be exploited in this way.

LATER ADOLESCENCE: AGES FIFTEEN TO SEVENTEEN

DEVELOPMENTAL TASKS

During later adolescence, teens begin to decrease their ego-centric view of the world and become less self-absorbed and self-conscious. Fenwick and Smith (1996) suggest that "parents gradually find that their child is becoming easier to live with." On the other hand, the older adolescents' quest for "finding themselves," for developing their unique identity, becomes a new challenge. In defining their own identity, they begin to seriously question everyone else's—especially their parents. Whether this need to build a unique sense of identity is as prevalent or difficult as is Erikson's traditional view of the adolescent "identity crisis" may be debated. Later teens move beyond puberty and toward adulthood with a desire to understand the world and their place in it by challenging anything that seems to be taken for granted. Stereotypical rebellious teenagers often have clarity about what they do not want or do not like, without necessarily knowing what they *do* want or like. This can become an endless frustration for parents, especially because their own values, traditions, and life decisions are being questioned by their children.

It is during later adolescence that many parents feel themselves fading into the background in their son's or daughter's life. Later adolescents may begin to form more serious romantic relationships in which they shift from believing the world revolves around them to believing the world revolves around their girlfriend or boyfriend. Going out with friends on weekends replaces family outings, and constant telephone calls seem to interrupt even informal chats, let alone meaningful conversations with parents.

But this does not mean your child's relationship with you is weakened, just changing. Though children may not want to admit it, they seek your support and approval now more than ever. They are simply enacting their increasing ability to articulate frustrations, tensions, needs, and opinions. After years of dependence on and acceptance of the authority and opinions of others (parents, siblings, teachers), they have found their own voice (Belenky 1986). Unfortunately, that voice is prone to drown out all others. In the excitement of realizing they have something to say, they may neglect to hear (or sometimes even acknowledge) the voices of anyone else, particularly those they have been listening to for so long (such as parents, siblings, and teachers). They listen to peers because they relate to them as cohorts living the same experience.

Jane Loevinger (Belenky 1986) believes that this rebellious voice is the logical stage that follows conformity to external rules that dominate the pre- and early adolescent experience. Challenging rules is an important step toward the adolescent's own self-awareness: their challenges to your beliefs and lifestyle are a way for them to begin to pull themselves out of being immersed and governed by them. Conversely, your observation may be that your teens are incredible conformists: you watch them walk down the street with their friends, sporting the same kinds of sneakers, clothes, and hairstyles. It is a time to conform with peers, rebel against parents.

Though it may sometimes feel hopeless and difficult, parents of later adolescents can help their children think through alternatives to the many aspects of life with which they may now find fault. Rechannel their energies away from negative views of others to develop positive views of themselves and their possibilities. Refrain from becoming defensive about your lifestyle, values, and life decisions.

Be open to the fact that they are developing personal identities of their own, which may be very different from your expectations. Celebrate the person your child is becoming, and try to value his or her differences from you. Use this as a "fresh chance to get to know your offspring" (Fenwick & Smith 1996). Take advantage of their new confidence in expressing their ideals by engaging in critical but supportive discussions with them about the consequences of their proposals.

CAREER PLANNING TASKS

Two major tasks happen simultaneously during this age period. While contemplating big plans for their long-term future, most adolescents discover short-term realities of everyday work through after-school and weekend jobs.

Part-time work. This work is different from the part-time work of the early adolescent in that it usually entails longer and more regular hours, and the young employee is subject to tax withholdings and regular workplace expectations. Typical jobs for later adolescents include store cashier, fast food server, health aide, and office assistant. Though studies have characterized these jobs as repetitive and routine, they provide the opportunity for enhanced self-respect, maturity, professionalism, financial responsibility (Elkind 1996), and the emotional intelligence capacities of empathy and perseverance.

Long-term plans. In line with the later adolescents' overall tasks of developing a unique identity and clarifying their life values is the work of exploring potential vocational identities. Eli Ginzberg (1979) called this the *tentative period.* "At about 15 or 16 adolescents begin to consider their values and look for occupations and activities that allow for the expression of those values. An interest in service to others is likely to arise at this time. They become more sensitive to the imminence of vocational commitment and finally, at about 17, begin to integrate interests, capacities, and values in a transition out of the tentative stage and into the realistic stage" (Fuhrman, 1986).

Donald Super also called this the *tentative substage* of career exploration, which "involves the consideration of needs, interests, capacities, values, and opportunities. Tentative choices are made and tried out in role-play, discussion, course work, and early jobs" (Montross & Shinkman 1992). The adolescent begins to identify appropriate fields and levels of work. Much research evidence supports the applicability of Super's theory to high school students (Holland 1995; Fuhrman 1986).

The pressure to make some of these longer-term decisions comes from deadlines for the *Scholastic Aptitude Test* (SAT®), college admissions processes, and scholarship applications for students planning to go on to higher education. One timetable suggests that students should contact a guidance counselor about college plans as early as tenth grade, begin visiting colleges and take the SAT by the spring of their junior year, and have applications into colleges of their choice by the winter term of twelfth grade.

Determining what to do after high school is perhaps one of the most important and stressful decisions a high school student has to make. It is no wonder that so many change majors or even colleges or decide not to go to college at all after high school because they hadn't decided what they wanted to do in time to meet admissions deadlines. Though times have changed since Ginzberg and Super introduced the notion of career exploration in order to proceed to higher education, a student still needs to make decisions about the overall direction of his or her career during later adolescence.

PARENTAL INVOLVEMENT

Given that this pressure for long-term decisions comes at a time of adolescent search for life meaning, peer conformity, and potential rebellion, parents should not be surprised if their child experiences periods of indecision, frustration, and changing interests and even declares that he or she refuses to participate in the process. The most crucial parental attribute during this period is patience. Hear your children out, listen to their reasoning and ideas, and help them contemplate the consequences of their potential decisions.

Interests exploration. Use the process suggested in Part Two of this book to help your children clarify their interests, skills, and values before they try to find colleges that will satisfy those needs. Too often students choose a college based on the enticing photos of the campus in its catalog. Location is a consideration, but the most critical attribute a college has is its academic program content. One way a student can match the content to his or her interests is to have a clear idea of what those interests are.

Part-time jobs. Help your children identify part-time opportunities that will give them an idea of what they may want to do full time. Though few people have aspirations for long-term work flipping burgers, a stint at a fast food counter makes sense if they are considering going into the food service industry or if they think they want to manage people and work directly with customers. If they are considering a health care profession, entry-level work at a local hospital or home health aide office is appropriate. If they think they want to work in a corporate environment, then an entry-level office job may be a logical first step.

Internships. In addition to regular part-time jobs, many companies offer summer internships and apprentice-type positions that will give an adolescent experience, a good work reputation, and credentials. High school guidance counselors are the best source of leads for these kinds of opportunities, as well as your own professional contacts and acquaintances. Introduce your child to contacts that may help her get started and help her learn how to conduct herself in an informational interview. See suggested resources in the Parent Tool Kit section.

CHRISTOPHER'S STORY

As he neared the end of his junior year of high school, Christopher was still very much undecided about his future plans. He seemed interested in many school subjects and had been involved in numerous extracurricular activities, but establishing any sort of sustained picture of what his future might be like continued to elude him. His parents knew that, like it or not, he would need to begin to get focused, as the time was rapidly approaching when Christopher would need to begin to identify a reasonable number of colleges to apply to. Neither of his parents had attended college, so their own ability to provide insight was somewhat limited. The guidance counselor, as best they could determine, was preoccupied with disciplinary problems and beyond a knowledge of a few colleges in the local area was unable to provide the depth of assistance needed.

Christopher's parents felt that they needed to retain the services of an educational consultant who could both help their son clarify what type of college might be best for him and assist in the process of identifying appropriate schools. They obtained the directory of certified educational consultants by calling the Independent Consultants Association as suggested by the guidance counselor and were able to identify three people in their area. They talked with all of them and had Christopher meet with two of them.

After making his choice, Christopher spent time with the consultant, and then all four of them met. The consultant was able to clarify what Christopher was looking for in a college; was then able to assist him in identifying five liberal arts colleges that offered the types of programs Christopher wanted; and finally worked with him and his parents to establish a timetable to visit each school, make an application, and in general guide them through the process.

Christopher found his work with the consultant extremely valuable. He received impartial and sound advice, which his parents had been unable to provide. Although still needing further clarification regarding long-term career plans, he felt very comfortable with the choice of college and highly motivated to move forward. His parents were likewise pleased that he had been able to make what seemed to be a well-reasoned decision.

Life balance. Finally, your child will need your help in thinking about how to balance the multiple demands of school, part-time work, and social relationships. Studies show that

adolescents who work more than fourteen hours a week tend to become cynical about work, spend less time on homework, are absent from school more often, do not participate in extracurricular activities, and spend less time with their families than adolescents who work less than fourteen hours per week. Since school is considered a full-time occupation, it makes sense that adolescents' work experiences should be limited, at least to the extent that they derive the maximum benefit from their school and school-related activities. (Fuhrman 1986)

Help your child budget time and balance his responsibilities.

WHAT NOT TO DO

Though your child may increasingly look and at times act like an adult, she is not as sophisticated as she or you may want to believe. "They still require the security of adult role models because during this period of rapid psychological and physical change, it is difficult to find internal direction. Adults have to provide the guidelines" (Elkind 1996). Her behavior may suggest (in fact, she may often say) she doesn't need you anymore. Don't believe her. She needs and appreciates your parental concern more than ever. The fine line continues between too much and too little involvement.

Your first reaction to many of your child's potential career directions may be immediate dismissal for all the right reasons, but with all the wrong consequences. You can't imagine your daughter going off to the city to become an actress. How many people try and fail? How would she make a living? How dangerous would it be to be alone in the city? However, instead of giving her the litany of reasons why it wouldn't work, explore the skills and attributes it would take to get there. Why does she think she would like doing that work? What outcomes would she hope to achieve? How would she earn a living while waiting for her big break? How else could she develop the talents she would need to really make it? Help her research and discover for herself the number of people who try and don't go through with their plans. Help her identify schools that would give her the skills she would

CHART 15

LATER ADOLESCENCE: AGES FIFTEEN TO SEVENTEEN

Developmental tasks
- Challenge rules, increase self-awareness
- Develop unique identity
- Become less self-absorbed and self-conscious
- Form more serious relationships

Career planning tasks
- Enter regular part-time work
- Identify tentative career choices, explore options
- Make decisions about college, post–high school plans

Parental involvement
- Discuss potential consequence of decisions
- Introduce to contacts, informational interviews
- Help them work through life balance issues—how to succeed at school, at work, and with social relationships

What not to do
- Do not dismiss their ideas for the future
- Do not force your ideas for colleges and majors
- Do not assume they no longer need your involvement

need, and ways she could finance her way through them. In the process of exploring the realities of pursuing a direction, she may come to the same conclusions you started with—but with a sense that you have supported her interests and are willing to work with her through these difficult decisions.

On the opposite side, many parents are quick to encourage their child toward the fulfillment of parent dreams and expectations that may or may not be in line with the child's interests. Help adolescents think through college plans, but don't force your ideas. Certainly share your opinions, but position them as such. Be clear about what you can afford to finance, but do not force ultimatums ("Go to my college or you're on your own"). If they choose a college out of your price range, help them work through financial aid options to supplement what you can afford to contribute.

Most important, help your children work through the career exploration process to identify their interests—and then identify higher education to match it—rather than looking at college choices based solely on financial or geographical considerations. If your son or daughter decides to forgo college immediately after high school, support that decision as well (with conversations about the consequences). Nowadays more students are electing to take some time off and work before going on to college—and for many it's the right decision.

10

STILL COACHING
AFTER HIGH SCHOOL
AND BEYOND

OME PARENTS WE TALKED TO when beginning to write this book assumed that career planning activities were only appropriate as a person prepares to leave the security of secondary education and move on to the world of work. Others assumed that a parents' guide would be geared toward younger children. In fact, your children are your children forever. Long after passing through milestones and rites of passage into adulthood, your offspring still look to you for parental support. This final age-related discussion encompasses the years when your child may no longer look and act like a child.

YOUNG ADULTHOOD: AGES EIGHTEEN TO TWENTY-TWO

We look at adulthood in two phases, young adulthood and later adulthood. The first period is referred to as young adulthood, though others may describe it as late or post-adolescence (Arnstein 1984).

DEVELOPMENTAL TASKS

Your children are your children forever. Long after passing through milestones and rites of passage into adulthood, your offspring still look to you for parental support.

The two main tasks of later adolescence—development of a unique separate identity, and strong relationships and connection with others—continue into young adulthood with greater intensity and focus. Beyond the struggle to conceptually identify their place in the world, many young adults begin to literally separate themselves from family environments and strike out on their own. Though some estimate that "up to 50 percent of 20–24 year olds continue to live with their parents today" (Elkind 1994), most young adults are either beginning the process or contemplating ways of moving on and developing a life of their own after they leave high school.

Age eighteen legally marks their entry into adulthood by granting them eligibility to vote and giving them responsibilities such as registering for the draft. If they plan to drive, most young adults obtain the right to do so by age eighteen, giving them a sense of freedom from dependence on their parents or others to help them get around. For those who go to college after high school, young adulthood is spent in an academic environment.

Erikson (1968) called young adulthood the crisis of intimacy versus isolation and noted the importance of developing interpersonal and romantic relationships. Many young adults form serious relationships and/or get married during this period, and some begin to raise families of their own. Many young adults begin new relationships with their parents, suddenly appreciating what has been done for them and how much support they have been given over the years.

Many parents develop a new appreciation for the person they have watched grow out of childhood and adolescence into a mature person they can relate to and confide in and with whom they can converse intelligently about serious issues (though they may often take different positions!). On the other hand, some young adults may withdraw even more from their immediate families in their quest for developing an independent life; their parents may experience the anxiety of not knowing where their children are, how they are doing, or with whom they are spending their time. Others wonder if their child will ever move on, and they dream of the "empty nest" that never seems to materialize.

CAREER PLANNING TASKS

In his early writings, Ginzberg (Montross & Shinkman 1992) identified the period past age seventeen as the time for realistic choice, when "the individual seeks for the last time to acquaint him or herself with alternatives. This is followed by the crystallization stage, when choices are determined, and finally by the specification stage, during which he or she makes them happen." During the 1970s, Ginzberg amended the notion that choices are final and irreversible when he suggested that though "early decisions have a shaping influence on careers, so do continuing changes of work and life. Occupational choice is a process that remains open as long as we make decisions about work and career" (Montross & Shinkman 1992). Though the changing employment contract enforces the nonpermanence of career decisions, young adulthood is a time when people begin to form clear direction and test out career alternatives. Super called this the later stages of the exploration stage, where young people explore alternatives through experience and experimentation.

It is during this time that people begin to form professional relationships with mentors, bosses, and colleagues. They begin to identify themselves with the work that they do. And they learn through trial and error not only what they want to do but what they do not want to do. Many older adults talk of the worst jobs of their lives coming at these times—factory positions or menial work in unsafe conditions. This may happen more for young adults who have foregone college and gone directly into the workforce, but higher education may bring them a stronger sense of what they do and do not want to do through internship opportunities or simply learning more about what they thought they wanted to do. Many young adults switch majors before graduating, as they become clear about their interests and skills. Still others may decide it is time to enter college after some time off in the "real world."

PARENTAL INVOLVEMENT

Whatever your children do after high school may be a challenge for you as a parent. If they are off to college, you may experience a sense of loss without their presence around the house. If they are still at home, you may wonder when they plan to leave and what they will do with themselves. If they have begun families of their own, you may worry how they will fulfill their new responsibilities. If you're not sure what they are doing, you may wonder whether they will ever take on responsibility. Although these are all legitimate worries, it is doubtful whether they are doing you or your young adult child much good.

The best thing you can do at this stage of your children's development is to listen to them, understand what they are doing and going through, and help support them toward their next steps. Welcome the assistance of alternative role models into their lives, especially professors and professional mentors. If career plans do not work out, encourage them to seek alternatives by revisiting their interests, skills, and values. Help them develop contingency plans. Celebrate successes with them, and share your pride and faith in their abilities. Encourage them to continue their education, but redefine education as continuous learning if college is not for them. Continue to help them think through the consequences of their decisions. If they do decide to live at home, give them responsibilities and obligations that will help them develop life skills. Help them identify career opportunities, and introduce them to colleagues who can help.

REBECCA'S STORY

Rebecca had enjoyed her first two years at college immensely. She had been able to dabble in a wide variety of academic areas due to the flexible requirements of the college. She had a wide range of academic and other interests, but no clear, sustaining career-related interest presented itself. Her parents began to be concerned that this lack of focus could cause frustration for Rebecca the following year and so encouraged her to visit the Career Services office when she began her junior year. Having listened to her friends who were seniors talk of the frustration of having to make hasty decisions as they approached graduation, she decided that her parents were right: now was the time to begin to sort out her postgraduation plans.

She made an initial appointment with one of the career counselors in the Career Services office, who suggested that she start by taking the *Strong Interest Inventory*, which would show her how her interests compared with those of happily employed people in more than one hundred career fields. The results confirmed what Rebecca had already suspected: she wanted to pursue career fields that would allow her to express herself creatively and would provide some challenge and financial reward. The counselor encouraged her to read *Real People, Real Jobs,* which contained interviews with people in artistic and other career fields. She found the interviews with the copywriter and the creative director of particular interest, although she had never before had an inkling of those career fields. Her parents, in the role of Connector, were able to put Rebecca in touch with an old friend who worked in the creative department of a large New York–based advertising agency. Rebecca conducted several informational interviews over the summer, which served to further spark her interest. The following year, she was able to get an internship in a smaller advertising agency near her college, which solidified her commitment. She continued to learn more about the field from alumni of her college who had provided their names to the Career Services office.

Rebecca's parents were pleased that she had received such valuable help through the Career Services office at her college. With their encouragement, and with the free services of the college's career counselor, Rebecca had gained considerable confidence in her future plans, and she appreciated the interest her parents had taken and the direct help they had provided.

WHAT NOT TO DO

Do not say "I told you so" if a career opportunity doesn't work out (even if you knew all along that it wasn't the right thing to do). Telling unmotivated children that they will never make anything of themselves will not motivate them; in fact, it will demotivate them and may turn into a self-fulfilling

CHART 16 **YOUNG** **ADULTHOOD:** **AGES** **EIGHTEEN TO** **TWENTY-TWO**	**Developmental tasks** ■ Attain independence ■ Develop intimacy ■ Create own family and lifestyle **Career planning tasks** ■ Complete high school ■ Attend college, enter into workforce ■ Form mentor relationships ■ Gain professional experience, identify with work ■ Learn about likes/dislikes through trial and error **Parental involvement** ■ Support decisions ■ Encourage contingency plans and ongoing development ■ Express pride and empathy ■ Welcome assistance of mentors and role models besides you **What not to do** ■ Don't say "I told you so" if something doesn't work out ■ Don't enable them to do nothing; encourage independence

prophesy. Help them identify what it is they could do and then support them as they try. At the same time, encourage independence: don't allow them to sleep all day and take advantage of your never-ending financial support.

Finally, remember whose career and life it is. This is not your chance to start over, though you still have the chance to do something different with *your* life!

LATER ADULTHOOD: AGES TWENTY-TWO AND OVER

The average age at which most people finally get settled into their careers is about age twenty-eight. As with all the information presented here, there are few hard and fast rules; some will make an appropriate career choice much earlier (research finds that interest in and aptitude for math and the sciences tend to develop relatively early), and others will continue to struggle to establish their career identities. In any event, the need for you to provide parental assistance does not end upon graduation from college or graduate school. In fact, the model presented in this book will provide a framework you can use over and over again as your child cycles through the four-stage decision-making process. In turn, you may find yourself drawing on your skills as a Clarifier, a Connector, a Challenger, and a Motivator well beyond the period in your child's life that you might have imagined.

DEVELOPMENTAL TASKS

As in all earlier stages of your child's growth and development, there are certain tasks relevant for people in this age range. Most important, your child will make her first entry into the adult world, and as we have seen in earlier chapters, that world is rapidly changing. If well prepared, she will be ready and able to operate in an ever-shifting workplace, where the emotional intelligence she developed much earlier will provide her with the internal strength to thrive. This initial shift from an academic setting can be difficult, a shift into a world where results are measured not by test results but by much more ambiguous measures.

For many, this is the start of the period that has been defined as becoming one's own person. This has meanings well beyond the scope of one's career, for it is during this period that one begins to establish oneself financially, socially, and as a member of a community. Implied as well here is the separation from one's family and the prospect of starting one's own.

CAREER PLANNING TASKS

Although for some the career tasks will focus on initial career success and getting well established, for many this is more a period of searching and settling. Despite his and your and others' best efforts, your son may come to realize that what looked like a good initial choice has turned out to be something other than anticipated. Working forty or fifty or more hours a week at something provides the only real test of whether or not it is a good fit. Expect some trial and error during this period. For some during this age, the simple desire to try something else, something different, is sufficient motivation to leave what in all respects is an attractive job. Turnover by young adults tends to be higher than normal in many organizations, not because of a bad boss or too many demands but simply because they feel a need to check out what may appear to be greener pastures.

This movement and searching may seem to you to be unwise, but it serves the important function of providing your adult child with additional data about herself and the world of work to analyze as she searches for that best fit. Your role here is to help her make moves that are supported by the data from the self-assessment rather than random moves simply for the sake of change. Although a few changes can add up to a compelling story, poorly thought-out moves can hinder career growth over time. However, if a career move helps your child gain insight and clarity, if it is part of a genuine effort to find the best fit, it may in the long run make sense; if so, support it.

All the career decision–making skills learned by your child in an earlier period will be needed whenever a change is required or sought. In today's and tomorrow's unsettled workplace, these skills may be called upon at any time, ready or not. Revisiting the self-assessment process is always an important step and one that should be encouraged at any transition point. The tools that you have introduced earlier may still play a helpful role here as the trial-and-error period continues.

PARENTAL INVOLVEMENT

Providing ongoing support and active listening can continue regardless of geographic distance. Assuming you have learned to assess where your child is in the career decision–

THE IMPORTANCE OF TEAMWORK

A recent study done at Bell Laboratories, the high-tech think tank . . . found that the most valued and productive engineers . . . were not those with the highest IQ, the highest academic credentials or the best scores on achievement tests. Instead, the stars were those whose congeniality put them at the heart of the informal communication networks that would spring up during times of crises or innovation.

New York Times,
September 10, 1996

making process (e.g., Is he really confused about a next step and therefore in need of some further self-assessment work, or is it more a question of needing help with identifying a few options to explore?), you can continue throughout this period to play the role of Clarifier, Connector, Challenger, or Motivator as is appropriate.

In addition to helping in those roles, you can also provide insight into the realities of the workplace. Help your child understand the importance of building and maintaining a network of people through whom she can gain support. Help her to seek out challenging assignments, which research has shown to be one of the most powerful ways to develop one's early career. Remind her that being smart is not as important as being an effective team member.

Another way to help is to encourage children to read some of the literature on what leads to success in one's career (see the Parent Tool Kit section for some suggestions). Regardless of career field, there are some common and commonsense practices that will help them get their career off to a sound start. Helping them understand that the informal rules are sometimes more important than the written ones; providing guidance on dealing with a difficult boss; and listening to their initial reactions to incompetence, self-serving colleagues, and corporate culture are all important ways that you can play a meaningful role during this sometimes difficult period.

CHART 17

LATER ADULTHOOD: AGES TWENTY-TWO AND OVER

Developmental tasks
- Leave the family
- Start out in the adult world
- Become one's own person
- Start a family

Career planning tasks
- Searchand settle
- Look for the "best fit"
- Get established in one's career field
- Gain clarity on one's career choice

Parental involvement
- Provide ongoing support
- Continue to act as Clarifier, Connector, Challenger, and Motivator as needed
- Help to make sense of the workplace
- Encourage those things that lead to long-term success

What not to do
- Do not expect that all is settled
- Do not push for quick solutions when things go wrong
- Do not disengage from providing help

If you have provided the necessary tools and sufficient love and caring, he will soon get on the right track and take off, happy in a career field well suited to his unique combination of talents.

WHAT NOT TO DO

It is not helpful at this time to become completely detached, any more than it is helpful to push for quick decisions. Knowing that this is a period of trial and error, do not encourage your adult child to stay with a job where he is obviously miserable or mismatched. Allowing him to move back home may be necessary in the short term, but do not make life so comfortable that he is not able to get on with the developmental tasks described above. Most of all, do not assign blame if things are not working out, and most especially if he has chosen a path that you did not find palatable in the first place. If you have provided the necessary tools and sufficient love and caring, have confidence that he will soon get on the right track and take off, happy in a career field well suited to his unique combination of talents.

11

OTHER CONSIDERATIONS
IN CAREER EXPLORATION

O ur purpose has been to provide a framework from which to approach the task of career coaching your kids, regardless of age and current stage of career discovery. We have looked at parental roles as they apply to the career steps of self-assessment, option finding, goal setting, and taking action, and have looked at age-appropriate activities to help children discover their career direction. We have encouraged you to think through your own career satisfaction and to find a balance between appropriate levels of assistance and overinvolvement in your child's career decisions. Our intention was to provide practical advice with a solid theoretical grounding.

There are many other directions to go beyond this introduction to career coaching for parents, and you will find in the final section a comprehensive "tool kit" of resources for additional reading and exploration. Career decisions are important and complex, and we acknowledge that we have not spent time delving into considerations such as the impact that disability, gender, ethnicity, racial identity, poverty, divorce, abuse, or even giftedness have on a child's career discovery process. People often think that a gifted child has all the opportunities in the world. But this "multipotentiality" increases the complexity of the decision-making process for gifted children—they have too many options from which to choose and often have little guidance because people assume they have the potential to do anything (Kerr 1990).

Research continues by many others into some of the unique barriers and opportunities for girls, minorities, and people with disabilities, and what we as both parents and society can do to address them. While we believe the steps and parental roles we have suggested hold true, we know that the scope of this book does not address some of the unique challenges felt by some children and parents more than others. Issues such as media influences, substance abuse, and standardized testing have a bearing on this discussion of career decision making, but they are also beyond the purview of this publication. Given that our experiences are primarily as counselors in the United States, we realize that beyond some of the research we have relied on from other countries, our perspectives are based on our North American experience. We do not assume that our recommendations will apply across the world without further investigation, and in fact know that in most parts of the developing world ideas surrounding work and careers are a different story.

We encourage you to continue the dialogue and exploration into these issues. The following lists are a small sample of the resources available to you across a broad range of additional issues to consider for career coaching your kids. We wish you and your children much success—and enjoyment—in the journey toward meaningful, satisfying careers.

RESOURCES IN PRINT

Adler, William M. (2000). *Mollie's Job: A Story of Life and Work on the Global Assembly Line.* New York: Lisa Drew Books.

Biller, E. F., & E. E. Horn (1991). "A career guidance model for adolescents with learning disabilities." *School Counselor, 38,* 279–286.

Callahan, K., J. A. Rademacher, and B. L. Hidreth (1998). "The effect of parent participation in strategies to improve the homework performance of students who are at risk." *Remedial and Special Education, 19,* 131–141.

Callahan, Michael J., and J. Bradley Garner (1997). *Keys to the Workplace: Skills and Supports for People with Disabilities.* Baltimore: Brookes Publishing.

Capuzzi, D., and D. R. Gross (1995). *Youth at Risk: A Resource for Counselors, Teachers, and Parents.* Alexandria, VA: American Counseling Association.

Ciulla, Joanne B. (2000). *The Working Life: The Promise and Betrayal of Modern Work.* New York: Three Rivers Press.

Driedger, Diane (2000). *Across Borders: Women with Disabilities Working Together.* Toronto: University of Toronto Press.

Geffert, Annette (2000). *A Toolbox for Our Daughters: Building Strength, Confidence, and Integrity.* Novato, CA: New World Library.

Granello, Paul F., and Fred J. Hanna (2003). "Incarcerated and court-involved adolescents: Counseling an at-risk population." *Journal of Counseling & Development, 81,* 11–18.

Hackett, G., and N. E. Betz (1981). "A self-efficacy approach to the career development of women." *Journal of Vocational Behavior,* 18(3), 326–339.

Harrington, Thomas F. (2003). *Handbook of Career Planning for Students with Special Needs.* Austin, TX: PRO-ED, Inc.

Hartley-Brewer, Elizabeth (2001). *Raising Confident Girls: 100 Tips for Parents and Teachers.* Cambridge, MA: Da Capo Press.

Hutchinson, Nancy L. (1993). "Career counseling of youth with learning disabilities." *ERIC Digest,* 800-LET-ERIC.

Hutchinson, Nancy L., J. G. Freeman, and C. Fisher (1993). *A two-year cohort study: Career development for youth with learning disabilities.* Paper presented at the annual meeting of the American Educational Research Association, Atlanta, GA.

Marone, Nicky (1998). *How to Mother a Successful Daughter: A Practical Guide to Empowering Girls from Birth to Eighteen.* New York: Harmony.

Miller, Alice (1994). *The Drama of the Gifted Child: The Search for the True Self.* New York: Basic Books.

Katz, Montana (1996). *The Gender Bias Prevention Book: Helping Girls and Women to Have Satisfying Lives and Careers (Gender in Crisis).* Northvale, NJ: Jason Aronson, Inc.

Kerr, Barbara (1990). "Career planning for gifted and talented youth." *ERIC ED Digest,* no. E492, ED 321 497.

Lapan, Richard T., Bradley Tucker, Se-Kang Kim, and John F. Kosciulek (2003). "Preparing rural adolescents for post–high school transitions." *Journal of Counseling & Development,* 3, 329–342.

Latinos at work. (series: *Latino Entrepreneurs; Careers in Community Service, ...Education, ...Entertainment, ...Law & Politics, ...Music Industry, ...Publishing &*

Communications, ... Science and Medicine, ...Sports). For grade 7 and up. Bear, DE: Mitchell Lane Publishers, Inc.

Louv, Richard (2003). "The superchild syndrome." www.connectforkids.com.

Minskoff, Esther, and David Allsopp (2003). *Academic Success Stategies for Adolescents with Learning Disabilities and ADHD*. Baltimore: Brookes Publishing.

Odean, Kathleen (2002). *Great Books for Girls: More Than 600 Recommended Books for Girls Ages 3–14*. (Rev. ed). New York: Ballantine Books.

Pasternak, Ceel, and Linda Thornburg (1999). *Cool Careers for Girls* (series). Manassas Park, VA: Impact Publications.

Pipher, Mary (1995). *Reviving Ophelia: Saving the Selves of Adolescent Girls*. New York: Ballantine Books.

Preparing Children for Adult Employment: Early Planning Is the Key (2003). Deerfield, IL: Hemophilia Galaxy.

Shandler, Sara (1999). *Ophelia Speaks: Adolescent Girls Write About Their Search for Self.* Perennial.

Shandler, Sara, and Nina Shandler (2003). *Ophelia's Mom: Women Speak Out About Loving and Letting Go of Their Adolescent Daughters*. New York: Three Rivers Press.

Smith, E. J. (1981). "The career development of young black females: The forgotten group." *Youth and Society, 12*(3), 277–312.

Stacy, Lori Moore (2000). *Discover Yourself (All About You)*. For ages 9–12. New York: Scholastic.

Tinajero, J. V. (1991). Raising career aspirations of Hispanic girls. *Fastback 320*. Bloomington, IN: Phi Delta Kappa Educational Foundation.

Wechman, Paul, and John Kregel (1998). *More Than a Job: Securing Satisfying Careers for People with Disabilities*. Baltimore: Brookes Publishing.

Weiler, Jeanne (1997). "Career development for African American and Latina females." *ERIC/CUE Digest,* no. 125. New York: ERIC Clearinghouse on Urban Education.

Wilson, Kimberly Lindsay (2000). *Work It! The Black Woman's Guide to Success at Work.* Campbell, CA: iUniverse Publishing Services.

Wolffe, Karen E. (1997). *Career Counseling for People with Disabilities: A Practical Guide to Finding Employment.* Austin, TX: PRO-ED, Inc.

INTERNET RESOURCES

Asian American Economic Development Enterprise	www.aaede.org
Asian American Job Search Engine	www.Asia.net
Aspira: An Investment in Latino Youth	www.aspira.com
The Black Collegian Online	www.black-collegian.com
The Black EOE Journal (searchable database)	www.blackeoejournal.com
Black Voices	http://new.blackvoices.com
BrassRing Diversity	www.brassringdiversity.com
Career Exposure	http://careerexposure.com
Diversity Careers	www.diversitycareers.com
Diversity Employment	www.diversityemployment.com
Diversity Job Bank	www.IMDiversity.com
Diversity Link	www.diversitylink.com
Equal Opportunities Publications, Inc. (EOP)	www.eop.com
Hire Diversity	www.HireDiversity.com

Hispanic Alliance for Career Enhancement	www.hace-usa.org
Hispanic Employment Service	www.saludos.com
Hispanic Online	www.Hispaniconline.com
Job Latino	www.JobLatino.com
Latino Opportunities	www.latpro.com
National Center on Workforce and Disability/Adult	www.onestops.info
Nativeweb	www.nativeweb.org
Nexus Research Group – Gifted Children	www.nexusresearchgroup.com/gifted_kids
Nontraditional Employment for Women	www.mnworkforcecenter.org
Quintessential Careers	www.quintcareers.com
Society for Advancement of Chicanos and Native Americans	www.sacnas.org
U.S. Department of Labor Office of Disability Employment	www.dol.gov/odep
US Hispanic Chamber of Commerce	www.ushcc.com
Women Work!	http://womenwork.org
Women Venture	www.womenventure.org
Work4women	www.work4women.org

PARENT TOOL KIT

FOR CAREER COACHING

We offer this final section as a summary of age-appropriate activity suggestions to correspond with the four career planning steps, some worksheets to get you started, and a selection of references. There are a wide variety of career development practitioners and materials—some outstanding, some mediocre, some that provide little or no value. We suggest the resources here as a guideline toward selecting the solution that's right for you and your child.

This book has introduced a process and tools for parents and their children to engage in career discovery together. We offer here a sampling of other resources that are available to parents in their roles relating to career coaching. On the following pages, you will find resources organized in the following categories:

CAREER COACHING YOUR PRESCHOOL KIDS

The following activities, exercises, and resources will help you in guiding your preschool kids.

SELF-ASSESSMENT: CLARIFYING INTERESTS, SKILLS, VALUES, AND PERSONALITY

Listen for clues about interests and personality. Do your preschool kids prefer introverted activities such as coloring, or playing with lots of other kids? Are they imaginative? Inquisitive? Messy or neat? What kinds of movies and characters do they like?

Encourage dress-up and fantasy games ("Let's pretend I'm a police officer"). Listen to and observe their perceptions of what people in different occupations do. Correct them if you hear misconceptions such as "Girls can't do that." Note the types of occupations they choose to "be."

Think about the types of toys they like and those that tend to end up at the bottom of the toy box. Imagine the connection between these interests and future possibilities.

EXPLORING OPTIONS: CONNECTING THEM WITH OPPORTUNITIES AND RESOURCES

Read picture books that show people in occupations: "Who's that?" Do we know anyone that does that?"

Suggest that they draw pictures of Mommy and Daddy at work and discuss your job with them. If you work outside the home, take them to work whenever possible so that they understand where you go and see that part of you (and see that work isn't a terrible place that steals you away).

As much as possible, expose them to a wide variety of people doing different jobs. Most people would welcome the chance to show a preschooler around their workplace. Encourage them to ask your family members and friends about what they do for a living and why they like doing that.

GOAL SETTING AND PLANNING: CHALLENGING THEM TO REACH FOR REALISTIC MILESTONES

Help them pick out a piggy bank and think about what they can save up to buy.

Give them their own age-appropriate tasks (such as cleaning up their toys) and praise them for doing a good job. Make a game of it ("Let's pretend you are a waiter and you can set the table"). Create a chores list and let them put stars on it as they complete each chore.

Keep an activities calendar and check off the days until a special event.

TAKING ACTION: MOTIVATING THEM TO PERSEVERE

Help them overcome discouragement if they cannot complete something they set out to do. Encourage them to try new things. Reward them with praise and encouragement when they do succeed.

Beware of language you use that may discourage future exploration based on your own likes and dislikes or on your knowledge of "reality." Children of this age require encouragement and imagination. Later you can help them set more realistic goals and milestones.

Remember that building emotional intelligence begins at an early age and will be foundational to your children's success regardless of the career paths they choose. Help them find positive ways to express their emotions, and be a role model of self-awareness and self-control.

WORKSHEET 1

CAREER COACHING YOUR PRESCHOOL KIDS

Have them draw a picture of what they want to be when they grow up.

Have them draw a picture of Mommy/ Daddy at work.

1. What are their favorite "pretend" games?

2. "Let's count how many different jobs we can find." (Make a game of identifying what family and community members do and note here observations about the ones your child seems intrigued by).

3. What are their favorite activities? What does that tell you about their personality preferences and interests?

4. Who are their favorite characters (in films, books, TV, etc.)? What does that tell you about the types of people/characteristics they admire?

CAREER RESOURCES FOR PRESCHOOL KIDS

PICTURE BOOKS ABOUT CAREERS

Kottke, Jan (2000). *A Day with a Mail Carrier* (Hard Work). Welcome Books.

Levin, James (2001). *What Will I Be?* Cartwheel Books.

Liebman, Daniel, and Dan Liebman (2000). *I Want to Be…* (series: *…a Police Officer, …a Pilot, …a Nurse*, etc.). Firefly Books.

Maynard, Christopher (1997). *Jobs People Do*. DK Books.

Rockwell, Anne, and Lizzy Rockwell (2000). *Career Day*. HarperCollins.

Simon, Norma (1998). *Fire Fighters*. Aladdin Library.

www.kids.gov. Web site for older preschool kids including Web treasure hunt of people in various careers.

BOOKS AND ARTICLES FOR PARENTS

Pruitt, David B. (1998). *Your Child: Emotional, Behavioral and Cognitive Development from Birth Through Preadolescence*. American Academy of Child & Adolescent Psychiatry. HarperCollins.

Understanding Your Young Child's Stages of Development. Child Welfare League of America. www.cwla.org.

White, Burton L. (1994, May). "Head start: Too little and too late: How a child develops in the first three years of life often determines success or failure in school." *Principal*, 13–15.

CAREER COACHING YOUR SCHOOL-AGE KIDS

The following activities, exercises, and resources will help you in guiding your school-age kids (ages six to twelve).

SELF-ASSESSMENT: CLARIFYING INTERESTS, SKILLS, VALUES, AND PERSONALITY

Most of us remember being asked the age-old question "What do you want to do when you grow up?" Keep the discussion going: "Oh, really? That's very interesting. Why would you want to do that?" Ask your kids to draw a picture of something they like to do at school, or outside of school, to show what they want to be when they grow up.

Continue to listen for clues about interests and encourage imagination. Note the consistency or differences in the types of play they liked when they were younger and the activities they enjoy today. Think about how they might someday translate these interests to future possibilities. A number of good books and computer games (outlined in this tool kit) are available for this age group to help them think through what they like and what they are good at, with simple comparisons of how those strengths might be used for different jobs.

While formal assessment processes are not necessarily applicable for this age, there is a version of the *Myers-Briggs Type Indicator* instrument made for children (the *Murphy-Meisgeier Type Indicator for Children*) available through a local career counselor. You can introduce older kids to the idea of career categories through assessments such as John Holland and Amy Powell's *SDS Career Explorer* and the *Harrington-O'Shea Career Decision-Making System*.

Talk with your middle school guidance office to understand what career exploration activities are available through the school. Volunteer to be a "Career Day" speaker. Understand any career curriculum being offered so that you can support it at home.

EXPLORING OPTIONS: CONNECTING THEM
WITH OPPORTUNITIES AND RESOURCES

Suggest that they do a school report on what a sample of people in your extended family and network do for a living. This will begin to develop informational interview skills and continue to expose them to a variety of workplaces and occupations. Encourage them to read biographies of a diverse range of people.

Many assessments link interests to lists of possible jobs. For areas your middle school children seem intrigued by, have them look up specifics in the *Young Person's Occupational Outlook Handbook.* See www.kids.gov for a free online overview "game" of career options for kids. A number of other online and CD-ROM-based career exploration games are also available.

Help older kids find "odd jobs" that match their expressed career interests if possible (e.g., if they think they might want to become a doctor or nurse, see if there are any opportunities in a hospital or physician's office).

GOAL SETTING AND PLANNING: CHALLENGING
THEM TO REACH FOR REALISTIC MILESTONES

School is job number one. Help them understand the connection between school and future success. Continue to help them develop emotional intelligence and social skills.

Begin providing an allowance and teach them money management skills. Help them open a bank account using their allowance and earned money from their odd jobs. Help them think about what they want and how to save for it.

TAKING ACTION: MOTIVATING THEM TO PERSEVERE

Keep them focused on their job as student. Teach them discipline (homework before play) and ensure they have the resources to succeed, such as a good night's sleep and proper nutrition. Don't be discouraged if they keep changing their mind about career direction. Kids discover career interests at different rates. Look for themes and connections to the interests they have previously expressed.

WORKSHEET 2

Have them draw a picture of what they want to be when they grow up. Why?

Have them draw a picture of them doing something they love to do.

CAREER COACHING YOUR SCHOOL-AGE KIDS

1. What types of gifts do they ask for? Do they prefer games and activities that involve many or do they prefer games that require concentration and quiet?

2. What are their favorite subjects at school? Which ones do they do best at? Which ones do they struggle to complete?

3. If you've done any type of career exploration using computer games, card sorts, or assessments, which type of work do they seem to prefer?

4. At this early stage, what types of careers can you imagine them wanting to pursue?

CAREER RESOURCES FOR ELEMENTARY AND MIDDLE SCHOOL STUDENTS

Bafile, Cara (2000). *Career Education: Setting Your Students on the Path to a Valued Vocation.* Education World. www.education-world.com.

Bowman-Kruhm, Mary. *A Day in the Life of...* (series: *...an Architect, ...a Veterinarian, ...a Coach, etc.*). For ages 9–12. Rosen Publishing Group.

Careers in Action. A series of hands-on kits designed to provide elementary students with an awareness of career clusters, typical job tasks performed, tools needed to do the job, and the training required. www.educationassociates.com/elementary.html.

Career Ideas for Kids... (series: *...Who Like Sports, ...Who Like Talking, ...Who Like Computers, etc.*). 12 volumes. Covers more than 100 occupations in 45 career awareness lessons. Ferguson.

Department of Labor (1999). *Children's Dictionary of Occupations.* Department of Labor.

Ferguson Career Biographies. 20 volumes. Stories of some of the world's most influential and admired people. Each book focuses on the subject's education and training, challenges on the job, mentors, and career achievements. Ferguson.

Harrington, Thomas F., and Arthur J. O'Shea (1998). *Career Decision-Making System Revised.* Career Interests Assessment. American Guidance Service.

Holland, John L., and Amy B. Powell (2001). *SDS Career Explorer (Self-Directed Search* interests assessment, young person's edition). Psychological Assessment Resources. www.parinc.com.

Maze, Stephanie. *I Want to Be...* (series: *...a Fashion Designer, ...an Astronaut, ...an Engineer, etc.*). Harcourt Paperbacks.

Jist Editorial Staff (2003). *Young Person's Occupational Outlook Handbook.* Career Communications, Inc. www.careerbookstore.com.

Ohio Department of Education (1998). *It's About Time: Parental Activities to Help Middle Grade Students Begin to Think About Career Choice.* www.ohiocareerdev.org.

Pasternak, Ceel, and Linda Thornburg (2003). *Cool Careers for Girls in... (series: ...Travel & Hospitality, ...Sports, ...Air and Space, ...Computers, ...Construction).* Career Communications Inc., www.careerbookstore.com.

Project Discovery. Hands-on guided instruction in a series of structured activities. Students perform real tasks of a worker in forty career fields, using that worker's actual tools, equipment, and materials. www.educationassociates.com/middle.school.html.

Reeves, Diane Lindsey, and Nancy Bond. *Career Ideas for Kids Who Like... (series: ...Math, ...Science, ...Animals, ...Computers, ...Writing, ...Art, ...Adventure).* Checkmark Books.

WISCareers.wise.edu. 800-442-4612. Includes software, books, videos, games, and books for elementary, middle, and high school levels. Software and games include:

Career Auction (middle, high)

Career Capers Adventure Game (elementary, middle)

Career Carnival (elementary, middle)

Dinocards, DinoFuture, Dinocolor, Dinodraw (elementary)

It's Your Future (middle)

Career Exploration Workbook (elementary, middle)

Children's Dictionary of Occupations Activities (grades 3–4, grades 5–6)

CAREER COACHING YOUR TEENS

The following activities, exercises, and resources will help you in guiding your teens.

SELF-ASSESSMENT: CLARIFYING INTERESTS, SKILLS, VALUES, AND PERSONALITY

Peruse some of the online self-assessment programs available. Have your teens print out their results and discuss their choices with you. If desired, now is the time you could consider a formal self-assessment such as the *Self-Directed Search*, MBTI, or *Strong Interest Inventory* instrument (available through a career coach).

Card sorts are a good way to help teens not only sort through what they like and want to pursue but also screen out the areas they want to avoid. Most are written at a level that even young teens can understand and help identify interests, skills, values, and potential occupations.

EXPLORING OPTIONS: CONNECTING THEM WITH OPPORTUNITIES AND RESOURCES

Encourage teens to volunteer and do community service projects that will give them visibility and experience in a field that interests them (e.g., in a local hospital or rest home, social services agency, school, chamber of commerce). This also strengthens their résumé and college grant applications.

Encourage them to be involved in clubs and extracurricular activities and to take elective courses that challenge them and continue to develop their skills and intellectual curiosity.

Discuss postsecondary plans early and often, and be a resource for helping them explore and narrow down their options. Help them expand their thinking beyond simply

"I want to go to college" to considering their career plans and interests first, followed by what education is required. If college is appropriate, help them seriously consider their major and what they want to learn. This will lessen the likelihood that they will struggle with changing majors or schools later, or leave college still without clear direction or the skills needed to follow their dreams.

Together explore opportunities for them to get into a formal mentoring, job shadowing, or apprenticeship program. If no formal programs exist through the school, check with local employers or the chamber of commerce. Check the online listings of internship opportunities in your geographic area. While most are geared toward college-age kids, many would probably consider older motivated teens.

GOAL SETTING AND PLANNING: CHALLENGING THEM TO REACH FOR REALISTIC MILESTONES

Encourage them to work part-time, again trying to match opportunities with future interests. Continue to emphasize the importance of school and grades and to help them hone money management skills. Discuss the dangers of debt (before credit card companies convince them otherwise!) and set and meet savings milestones.

Help them identify realistic short-term job alternatives for longer-range goals (e.g., work as a law clerk while dreaming of owning their own firm; work in a nonprofit agency while studying social work). Encourage them to explore tools such as the *Young Person's Occupational Outlook Handbook* and online activities to learn more about occupations of interest.

Together create a list of people they can interview to find out more about jobs and college choices they may be considering. See the Informational Interview Packet (www.cbc2. org/c_access/interpak.html) for tips on how to contact an employer, conduct the interview, and follow up and document the experience.

TAKING ACTION: MOTIVATING THEM TO PERSEVERE

Emphasize the importance of deadlines and persistence in the postsecondary decision-making process. Work with their school to understand financial aid and application processes. Don't do the work for them—but make sure they do it!

WORKSHEET 3

**CAREER
COACHING
YOUR TEENS**

Ask your teens to create a collage that depicts them now and ten years from now, using photos from magazines, drawings, etc.

1. Do they still like to draw, doodle, draw cartoon characters and "graffiti" images? Do they like to take things apart and build things, like their bicycles or first cars?

2. What feedback do you receive from teachers? How would their friends describe them? What words would you use to describe their strengths?

3. If they've done card sorts, assessments, or online career exploration, what styles, values, and interests have they expressed so far? What types of careers have they explored and are considering pursuing?

4. Given their interests and aspirations, what type of postsecondary experience are they considering?

   ▪ 4-year college
   ▪ 2-year college
   ▪ Tech prep or apprenticeship program
   ▪ Military
   ▪ Work experience/On-the-job training
   ▪ Other

5. List the jobs, internships, and volunteer work they've done and how well they've done at them. List people they should/did meet with for informational interviews. What did they learn?

CAREER RESOURCES FOR
HIGH SCHOOL STUDENTS

Andrews, Suzanne et al.(1998). *It's the 11th Hour in Your Teen's High School Career! Do You Know Where Your Kids Are Going?* Ohio Department of Education. www.ohiocareerdev.org.

Bingham, Mindy, Judy Edmondson, and Sandy Stryker (1994). *Choices: A Teen Woman's Journal for Self-Awareness and Personal Planning.* Advocacy Press.

Brain, Marshall (1997). *Part-time Jobs* for *Teenagers.* In *The Teenagers Guide to the Real World.* BYG Publishing. 2003 online excerpt available at www.bygpub.com.

Careers for You (series). Fifty in-depth descriptions of careers for animal lovers and car buffs to careers for talkative types and night owls. From Career Communications, Inc. www.careerbookstore.com.

Covey, Franklin (2003). *How to Help Your Teen Get Excited About College or a Vocation.* www.franklincovey.com.

Davis, Jim (2003). *Learning to Fail Successfully.* Career Resource Center for Families. www.familycorner.net/careerhelp/fail_successfully.htm.

Jobe, Hazel (2000). *Mapping Your Future.* Online site for grades 9–12. www.education-world.com.

Louv, Richard (2003). *The Superchild Syndrome.* www.connectforkids.org.

Patenaude, Alice (2003). *The Financial Aid Puzzle: Avoiding Financial Aid Foibles.* Teenagers Today. http://teenagerstoday.com/resources/articles/finaid.htm.

Phifer, Paul (2000). *College Majors and Careers: A Resource Guide for Effective Life Planning* (4th ed.). Ferguson.

Schilling, Dianne, Pat Schwallie-Giddis, and W. James Giddis (2003). *Preparing Teens for the World of Work.* Cord Communications. www.cordcommunications.com.

Stepp, Laura Sessions (2000). *Our Last Best Shot: Guiding Our Children Through Early Adolescence.* Riverhead Books.

Vernon, Naomi (2003). *A Teen's Guide to Finding a Job.* 1stBooks Library.

Zielin, Lara (2003). *Make Things Happen: The Key to Networking for Teens.* Lobster Press.

Make High School Count. Good online links and references and online career and educational planning tools beginning in 8th grade. http://mapping-your-future.org

www.collegeboard.com. Good overall site for high school students. Includes articles such as *"Action Plan: Freshmen: What Should You Be Doing Right Now?"* (overview of SAT requirements and deadlines); *"Volunteer Opportunities: Helping Others Help You"; and "Taking Time Off After High School."*

CAREER COACHING YOUR ADULT CHILDREN

Use the following activities and suggestions in guiding your adult children.

SELF-ASSESSMENT: CLARIFYING INTERESTS, SKILLS, VALUES, AND PERSONALITY

If they have not already done so, encourage your adult children to complete self-assessment activities such as motivated card sorts, the *Strong Interest Inventory* assessment, the *Self-Directed Search*, or an online assessment process. Suggest that they get some professional assistance from a school counselor or career coach.

If they have realized what they do *not* want to do (e.g., they want to change their major in college or change an unsatisfying job), help them analyze what about that experience they did not like and what they did. They may be in the right field but the wrong job or academic program, or they may need to rethink their direction altogether. It's important to know the difference before jumping to conclusions.

Remind them of some of the activities they showed interest in when they were younger and recollect some of your earlier discussions. Share your earlier observations of apparent interests and talents, being careful not to steer them in a direction you always wished they would go but they still have not.

EXPLORING OPTIONS: CONNECTING THEM WITH OPPORTUNITIES AND RESOURCES

Work with them on the computer to explore job search sites and to uncover the "hidden job market." Help them think beyond their geographic area by exploring transportation and housing alternatives.

If they are employed but feel stuck and have reached a dead end, help them strategize how to negotiate for better pay or increased opportunities. If they like the work but not the work environment, help them think through ways to improve their morale or to find a different situation.

If they are established in their chosen career but out of work, help them identify professional groups and networking opportunities in fields that interest them. Encourage them to join associations and to consider publishing articles in their field for increased visibility.

GOAL SETTING AND PLANNING: CHALLENGING THEM TO REACH FOR REALISTIC MILESTONES

Help them balance their desire to "start at the top" with the need to gain valuable experience and consistent income. Suggest they consider nontraditional alternatives such as temporary or contract work, freelance opportunities, or a combination of internships in their field of interest supplemented with paid work in perhaps an unrelated field while working toward a full-time position.

Encourage them to set specific time-framed goals and milestones. If they are working toward a long-term goal, remind them that every step is leading them closer. At the same time remind them that detours sometimes lead to a better unexpected place and they should not be afraid to take a risk when a new opportunity presents itself.

TAKING ACTION: MOTIVATING THEM TO PERSEVERE

If they are job searching, help them create a plan and schedule so that they stay focused and active rather than sitting back and feeling bad about being unemployed (or feeling too comfortable saying they can't find a job). Remind them that it takes time and energy but that every activity (even failed interviews) moves them further toward success.

Encourage them to take full advantage of career resources available to them, such as college career services (e.g., internships, counseling, alumni listings, etc.) or outplacement and unemployment services if they have experienced a layoff.

If you let them get away with doing nothing, they will be happy to oblige. Make sure they know that no-cost living at home is not a lifelong option!

WORKSHEET 4

**CAREER
COACHING
YOUR ADULT
CHILDREN**

1. Why are they in need of your coaching and support? Is it because they

   - Still haven't decided what to do after high school (not working or working at a trivial, unsatisfying job)?
   - Are in college and need continued support?
   - Are in college and want to change direction?
   - Are finishing college and looking for work/next steps?
   - Are going back to work after having a child?
   - Are working but unsatisfied?
   - Are at risk of losing their job due to downsizing?
   - Lost their current job (laid off, fired, quit)?
   - Other?

2. How engaged were you in their career decision making in the past? Did you follow a process similar to that outlined in this book—i.e., did you discuss their interests, help them discover options, etc.? How involved have you been along the involvement continuum (see page 14)?

   - Too involved: may have overinfluenced them and have to make sure now that you're helping them make the discovery for themselves
   - Appropriately involved: this will be an extension of a good, healthy relationship and ongoing career coaching process
   - Not involved enough: this will be a beginning for both of you

3. What help do they want from you? What do you think you can provide?

4. From working through card sorts, online assessments, a career counselor, or discussion and observations, in what general areas are they looking for work? What are their interests, values, and criteria for a successful work experience?

5. Who could potentially help them in their career exploration or job search?

6. Help them create a plan:

   - Identify interests, skills, values
   - Determine potential job areas or alternative college majors to explore
   - Search for opportunities and additional information
   - Update résumé, practice interviewing techniques
   - Take action: explore, send résumés, interview, get the job

CAREER RESOURCES FOR COLLEGE STUDENTS AND JOB CHANGERS

Bolles, Richard N. (1999). *How to Deal with Being Fired.* www.jobhuntersbible.com/library/nunters/fired.shtml

Duncan, Henrietta (1994, March–Apr.). "Graduation: no job offer yet—what now?" *Black Collegian,* 24(4), 65.

Hall, Colin, and Ron Lieber (1996). *Taking Time Off: Inspiring Stories of Students Who Enjoyed Successful Breaks from College and How You Can Plan Your Own.* Penguin Books.

Knowdell, Richard. Revised editions of card sorts including Motivated Skills, Career Values Kit, and Occupational Interests Kit. Available from www.careertrainer.com, 800-888-4945.

Lorber, Laura (2003). "HR Managers forecast an upbeat hiring outlook." *Wall Street Journal.* www.careerjournal. com.

Montross, David H., Zandy B. Leibowitz, and Christopher J. Shinkman (1995). *Real People, Real Jobs: Reflecting Your Interests in the World of Work.* Davies-Black Publishing.

Noble, David F. (2000). *Gallery of Best Resumes* (2nd ed.). Jist Works.

O'Connell, Brian (2002). *The Career Survival Guide.* Career Communications, Inc. www.careerbookstore.com.

Peterson, Linda (1995). *Starting Out, Starting Over: Finding the Work That's Waiting for You.* Davies-Black Publishing.

Sullivan, Robert (1995, Feb. 23). "Making money the old fashioned way (college graduates in blue collar jobs)." *Rolling Stone,* 5(702), 53.

Tieger, Paul T., and Barbara Barron-Tieger (2001). *Do What*

You Are: Discover the Perfect Career for You Through the Secrets of Personality Type (3rd ed.). Little, Brown and Company.

Westover, Jeff (2003). "The reality of virtual networking." www.careermag.com/JS/General/catalog.asp.

www.rpi.edu/dept/cdc/student/careeropps.html. Lists and links relating to career choices upon graduation for various college majors.

CAREER SERVICES FOR MIDDLE AND HIGH SCHOOL STUDENTS

A range of career services are available to junior high and high school students. The quality and breadth of these vary tremendously, and it is important that you and your child become familiar with what is (and what is not) available. Following are the common resources.

GUIDANCE COUNSELORS

When helping your child with career planning, expect to find a wide range of competence and interest available. Some guidance counselors are excellent in this area, devote time to it, and have the types of resources outlined below. Others may not be as skilled or have the time and resources. Most are stretched quite thin with other responsibilities. Many school districts have dedicated time and resources to career education and have people dedicated to career development initiatives. Some school systems, such as the Ohio Department of Education, have a formal career planning process that begins in middle school and continues through senior year. This is obviously the most beneficial type of process, but unfortunately many schools still begin focusing on career interests in the eleventh or twelfth grade when it is time to think about postsecondary choices. We suggest you meet the guidance counselors, partner with them to the extent they are able, and encourage your children to avail themselves of whatever is at hand.

COMPUTER-BASED CAREER PLANNING SYSTEMS

Career and College Quest, from Peterson's (see p. 210), is an example of a software package designed to assist high school students in identifying career alternatives, colleges, and vocational programs. It also provides financial aid options. Other features include self-assessment of interests, skills, and personal style; 1,000 job descriptions; information on more than

3,200 two- and four-year colleges; electronic applications that can be sent directly to admissions officers; "campus visits" via a CD feature; and financial aid worksheets.

There are numerous such systems. Check with your school guidance office to determine if one is available. However, even the most sophisticated computer-based system cannot provide all the answers. Work in partnership with the guidance counselor to get maximum benefit from the system. For more detailed information on the most commonly available systems, contact the organizations below.

DISCOVER®
ACT, Inc.
Educational Services Division
P.O. Box 168
Iowa City, IA 52243
319-337-1000

Occupational Outlook on Computer
CFKR Career Materials, Inc.
11860 Kemper Road #7
Auburn, CA 95603
800-525-5626

Modular C-LECT
Chronicle Guidance Publications, Inc.
66 Aurora Street
Moravia, NY 13118
800-622-7284

Coin Educational Products
3361 Executive Parkway, Suite 302
Toledo, OH 43606
800-274-8515

SIGI PLUS® Program
Educational Testing Service
Rosedale Road
Princeton, NJ 08541
800-257-7444

Quest
Peterson's
200 Lenox Drive
P.O. Box 67005
Lawrenceville, NY 08648
609-896-1800 or 877-433-8277

The Guidance Information System (GIS)
Riverside Publications
8420 Bryn Mawr Avenue
Chicago, IL 60631
800-323-9540

INTERNSHIPS

Internships may vary in terms of length, breadth, and depth, but you should encourage your child to take advantage of them as they are available. One of the very best methods of career exploration is getting exposure to a potentially interesting career field to see how it feels. Some resources to learn about internships and internship possibilities include:

- www.thehighschoolgraduate.com. A good overview of internships and how to choose one that matches your interests and skills. Also includes information about job shadowing and college search.

- Internshipprograms.com, http://internships.wetfeet.com/. Includes a searchable database for candidates looking for internship opportunities.

- www.ams.org/employment/internships.html. Listing of major companies throughout the U.S. that offer internship programs for high school and college students.

VOLUNTEER WORK

Another important option is community service and volunteer work, which can begin in middle school and continue for a lifetime. Not only do students get valuable experience, referrals, and visibility into the world of work, they also gain the satisfaction and selflessness that comes from giving back to the community, and community members and agencies benefit from the volunteer work that they do. Check with your local senior center, hospital, social service agency, or city hall. There is never a shortage of opportunities for community service and volunteer work. Some additional resources to identify volunteer opportunities for high school and beyond include:

- Serve Net, www.servenet.org

- Action Without Borders, Idealist.org

- Peace Corp, www.peacecorps.gov/indexf.cfm

- Internet Nonprofit Center, www.nonprofits.org/

SCHOOL-TO-CAREER PROGRAM SYSTEMS

An innovative approach now operating in many states includes school-to-work or school-to-career programs, which receive federal support via the School to Work Opportunity Act, and other workplace learning programs sponsored by the Workforce Investment Act and state-funded job training programs. Although there are variations at the local level, a typical system combines the efforts of schools, businesses, colleges, labor, and other parties. Components of the program might include work-based learning (shadowing and internship experiences), school-based learning (applied learning, career counseling and assessment), and "connecting activities" such as matching students and employers. Check with your guidance counselor to determine if such a program is operating in your area.

OTHER PROGRAM RESOURCES

Individual school systems may have developed unique and innovative programs to serve the career needs of their students.

A visit with the guidance office will help you identify these programs and resources. If none exists at the moment, consider suggesting some activities and volunteering to help with them, such as coordinating career days or field trips to local employer sites. Check with the local chamber of commerce to inquire about employer-sponsored internships and career awareness programs.

WORKING WITH AN EDUCATIONAL CONSULTANT

Independent educational consultants provide assistance in four areas:

SCHOOL

Serves students in grades 1 through 12 and postgraduate year and may serve younger children. Such placements often focus on private day and boarding schools; may include summer placements.

COLLEGE

Serves those applying for undergraduate admission; may serve graduate and professional school applicants; may include summer placements of college students.

SPECIAL NEEDS

Serves those of all age levels with emotional or behavioral difficulties—as well as those with unique mental or physical requirements—who need educational placement.

OTHER

Serves clients with a variety of other needs such as overseas placement, foreign student advisement, crisis intervention, career counseling, summer program identification, and vocational counseling.

To obtain a free listing of IECA-certified consultants by state and area of specialty, contact the Independent Educational Consultants Association, www.iecaonline.com, 800-808-IECA or 703-591-4850, e-mail IECA@aol.com, fax 703-591-4860.

According to the material received from the IECA, a professional association of people doing this work, consultants "provide unbiased advice and recommendations based on their professional judgment of a student's needs and abilities." We contacted one of their consultants, who gave us this description of their work:

> We are essentially macro educators to our students and to their families. Although we enter their lives as they go through the college admissions process, we are concerned with more than college placement. Our focus is upon preparation for life. On the immediate side, we serve as objective college counselors, sometimes as mediators, and often as sounding boards for our clients' ideas or for notions they have picked up from others. Essentially, however, we strive to raise their thinking to a higher, broader level, to maximize our students' long-term potential.
>
> Foremost, our value lies in our ability to be good educators, to enable our students to understand what is most important about them in a lifelong educational context. When they are high school students, we focus upon their four-year academic programs. We teach them what course selection tells colleges about applicants and what value particular courses hold for students in terms of preparation for college, for graduate school, and for careers. We also concern ourselves not just with the content of curriculum but also with whether or not our students are learning to think. Do they want to write well? Do they want to know the English language in depth? Are they maximizing their quantitative potential? Do they like to read? What do they like most academically? Are they fulfilling their own interests?
>
> Of course, the colleges already have the answers to these questions about them, which leads us to our candidates' ability to present themselves—to articulate who they are. We enter this arena by creating simulated interviews in which we probe our students to think maturely and intellec-

tually to enable them to crystallize and to articulate what is most important about themselves, academically and personally. We also probe their social perspective, which brings us to the surface issues of integrity and social responsibility.

There also exists the pragmatic side of our service—how to market the individual's specific talents such as achievement in athletics and the arts. But regardless of our candidates' extracurricular abilities and accomplishments, when it comes to admissions committees, the focus shifts to the quality of the mind, to how well it has been developed.

Therefore, we teach our students how to sell themselves, personally and intellectually, by interviewing effectively and by writing mature essays. For instance, students typically start responses to questions with negative statements. In contrast, we teach them to concentrate on their positive thoughts about themselves and their experiences. We also teach them to focus on what is most important. I have often heard college admissions officers advise students to "simply be yourselves," to "speak from the heart." I agree that it is important for applicants to present their true selves. To be fair to themselves, however, they are wisest when they first think carefully about their own values and views. If you tell adolescents to allow any idea to flow out of themselves that happens to surface at the moment, without careful preparation, the risks are considerable that they will not present their best or truest thoughts.

Our students, therefore, are prepared before they present themselves to their evaluators. They also possess a plan of what they want to get out of college, although they usually do not know precisely the form their future careers will take. In addition, we hope they will feel that they turned over every possible stone to get their first-choice college, while in the process learning to think deeply, maturely, and clearly.

Dunbar Educational Consultants, Inc.
Brookline, MA, and Fairfield, CT

TOP TEN THINGS RISING SENIORS CAN DO THIS SUMMER TO GET A JUMP ON THE COLLEGE SEARCH

In a May 2002 survey, the members of the Independent Educational Consultants Association (IECA) listed the top things rising seniors can do to get a jump on the college search.

1. **Write a generic admission essay.** Applying for college can take up as much time as a regular class during the senior year. By preparing a generic essay in advance that can be tailored to different applications, the student can spend more time on studies and extracurricular activities once school begins.

2. **Complete one college admission application.** This application can serve as the prototype for all other applications. The Common Application is accepted by hundreds of colleges and may be a good place to start.

3. **Collect reference letters.** Normally reference letters come from junior year teachers who have taught the student for the last full year. Teachers usually appreciate having the extra time over the summer to write a reference when the memory of the student's achievements is fresh.

4. **Visit (or plan to visit) campuses.** While summer is not the ideal time to visit campuses because there aren't many students there, this is the time high school students are free and parents' schedules are usually more flexible. These visits can also be made in the early fall and should include sitting in on a class, looking at the dorm rooms, eating in the cafeteria, and meeting with coaches and professors in areas of interest.

5. **Develop a preliminary list of colleges.** Call, write, or use the Internet to request information. Some colleges may even give out names of alumni in the student's neighborhood who may be willing to share experiences. Use this information to create a list of colleges to apply to.

6. **Participate in interesting activities.** Summer is a time to act on interests through internships, volunteer work, clubs, or paid positions. Try something productive and creative, preferably in an area of interest.

7. **Keep a summer journal.** A journal can help students chronicle their activities as well as determine what they want and need for the next few years. Journals also serve to help improve communication skills, critical for later success.

8. **Plan to take the SAT®, ACT, SAT II.** Rising seniors should have taken SATs and ACTs at least once by this point, but they may want to look at them when they're offered again in the fall. Those taking SAT II subject tests will need to decide which subjects to take. If SAT prep courses are planned, sign up now for early fall.

9. **Begin scholarship search.** Use books and Web-based services to begin a search for private money.

10. **READ!** IECA experts point to reading as the best way to improve vocabulary and prepare for standardized tests. While reading, have a dictionary handy to look up unfamiliar words.

IECA is a professional association of full-time experienced independent educational consultants who work with families on school placement issues. For more information on IECA, visit www.IECAonline.com or call 703-591-4850.

CAREER SERVICES FOR COLLEGE STUDENTS

CAREER COUNSELING

Over the past decade or more, colleges have increased the quality and quantity of career counseling available to their students. Most notably at liberal arts colleges, where the college-to-career connection is less clear, students now have available to them professionally trained career counselors. Students who are undecided about their career plans should visit with a career counselor well before their senior year.

TESTING

A variety of vocational/career interest, skill, and personality assessments should be available in the career counseling office, or the counseling center, which is more likely staffed with psychologists. Some of the better-known interest assessments are the *Strong Interest Inventory* instrument; the *Self-Directed Search*; and the *Campbell Interest and Skill Survey*. The *Myers-Briggs Type Indicator* (MBTI) instrument is widely available in college counseling centers and is an excellent personality assessment instrument (see Chapter 4 for more details).

COMPUTER-BASED CAREER PLANNING TOOLS

As is true at the junior and senior high school levels, there are numerous computer-based career planning systems designed for college populations, including SIGI and DISCOVER. Although these tools may be very helpful, they are not sophisticated enough to answer all the questions associated with career decision making.

We recommend a blended approach. Users should take advantage of online tools to get started, followed by reading and discussions with qualified counselors who can help interpret results and help the user think through next steps. College students should start with their career services office to see what professional online tools are available. Be cautious of some Internet-based "tests"—opt instead for tools that have been validated and recommended by career professionals. Remember that these are not "tests" but assessments that provide information based on how the person answers them. Only the user can validate the results.

ALUMNI NETWORKS

One of the single best resources available to your college-age children is the listings of alumni who have volunteered to assist with providing everything from informational interviews to assistance with finding summer employment or internship experiences to job placement help. Be sure that your children avail themselves of this "instant network," which will provide them with a resource all job hunters treasure.

WORKSHOPS AND CAREER FAIRS

Encourage your children to take advantage of all relevant workshops and/or career fairs, which will provide good information about themselves and the world of work. It is difficult to get this much firsthand information elsewhere. Again, urge them to attend these sessions well before their senior year.

ON-CAMPUS RECRUITING

Mostly for seniors, and limited for the most part to large corporations (the few exceptions might include a recruiting visit from the Peace Corps or other nonprofit organization), this is an invaluable time-saver and a great convenience for seniors. Underclass students should attend informational sessions sponsored by these organizations to begin to understand what they are looking for in terms of majors, GPA, and other factors.

CAREER SERVICES HOME PAGE

Many career services offices have established a home page on the World Wide Web that allows students twenty-four-hour access to job listings, recruiting schedules, or lists of services. The career office home page may also link to other job search resources available on the Internet.

INTERNSHIPS/EXTERNSHIPS

Internships and similar programs are strongly encouraged, especially for liberal arts students, who will need all the relevant experience they can acquire before graduating. Although these programs are allocated in various ways (some for academic credit, some not; some for majors only, some not), they all provide invaluable opportunities to get firsthand experience, good or bad, which will inform the career decision–making process.

CAREER LIBRARY

Most colleges now have excellent collections of career-related reading and reference materials available. Again, encourage your children to visit the career library well before their senior year, where they will find everything from books on self-assessment to addresses of potential employers. Also encourage them to spend time on the online sites noted throughout this tool kit to familiarize themselves with the many resources available to them.

RÉSUMÉ-WRITING SERVICES

This is a great service that should be taken advantage of while in school. It is probably good for a sophomore to explore this area rather than wait until senior year only to find that he or she has nothing much to write about. Résumés provide a framework that has uses well beyond employment applications. Asking students to write a résumé encourages them to think through their skills, qualities, and career objectives. It also provides incentive for them to do some of the activities that will be good for their career in the long run but which may seem to them to have no immediate return—for example, unpaid internships and volunteer work. Their first thought may be "How much will this pay?" But equally important questions are "What will I learn from this?" and "Will this look good on my résumé?"

GRADUATE SCHOOL ADVISING

Although the percentage of students going directly on to graduate school fluctuates, your child should take advantage of this expert advice in the selection of any graduate program. This obviously is a major career decision and thus merits careful planning and attention.

WORKING WITH A CAREER COUNSELOR

The National Career Development Association, a division of the American Counseling Association, provided the following consumer guidelines for selecting a career counselor.

ROLES OF THE CAREER COUNSELOR

Services of career counselors differ depending on the counselor's level of competence, the setting, client needs, and other factors. National Certified Career Counselors and other professional career counselors help people make and carry out decisions and plans related to life/career directions. Strategies and techniques of professional career counselors are tailored to the specific needs of the person seeking help. It is likely that the career counselor will do one or more of the following:

- Conduct individual and group personal counseling sessions to help clarify life/career goals

- Administer and interpret tests and inventories to assess abilities, interests, and other factors and to identify career options

- Encourage exploratory activities through assignments and planning experiences

- Utilize career planning systems and occupational information systems to help individuals better understand the world of work

- Provide opportunities for improving decision-making skills

- Assist in developing individualized career plans

- Teach job-hunting strategies and skills and assist in the development of résumés

- Help resolve potential personal conflicts on the job through practice in human relations skills

- Assist in understanding the integration of work and other life roles

- Provide support for persons experiencing job stress, job loss, and career transitions

CAREER COUNSELOR TRAINING AND CREDENTIALS

The designation National Certified Career Counselor signifies that the career counselor has achieved the highest certification in the profession. Furthermore, it means that the career counselor has

- Earned a graduate degree in counseling or a related professional field from a regionally accredited institution

- Completed supervised counseling experience that included career counseling

- Acquired a minimum of three years of full-time career development work experience

- Successfully completed a knowledge-based certification examination

Professional career counselors may also be trained in a one- or two-year graduate-level counselor preparation program with a specialty in career counseling. They may be licensed by state agencies or certified by national or state professional associations.

WHAT CAREER COUNSELORS DO

The services of career counselors differ depending on competence. National Certified Career Counselors or other professional career counselors help people make decisions and plans related to life/career directions. The strategies and techniques are tailored to the specific needs of the person seeking help.

CAREER COUNSELING FEES

Select a counselor who is professionally trained, who specifies fees and services upon request, and who lets you choose the services you desire. Make certain you can terminate the services at any time, paying only for services rendered.

PROMISES

Be skeptical of services that make promises of more money, better jobs, résumés that get speedy results, or an immediate solution to career problems.

ETHICAL PRACTICES

Professional career counselors are expected to follow the ethical guidelines of organizations such as the National Career Development Association, the National Board of Certified Counselors, the American Counseling Association, or the American Psychological Association. Professional codes of ethics advise against grandiose guarantees and promises, exorbitant fees, breaches of confidentiality, and related matters of misconduct. You may wish to ask for a detailed explanation of services offered, your financial and time commitments, and a copy of the ethical guidelines used by the career counselor or service you are considering.

A list of National Certified Career Counselors in your area may be obtained from the National Board of Certified Counselors (NBCC) at 910-547-0607. You can conduct an online search for certified counselors in your area at www.nbcc.org. Also see listings in your yellow pages or contact your local library for listings of college services, adult education programs, state employment agencies, and vocational rehabilitation programs. For more information, see Juliet V. Miler, "How Do I Find a Career Counselor?" *Career Developments*, 12(1), September 1996. For additional sound advice on selecting a career counselor for your children (or to help them make that decision), see part 3 of *What Color Is Your Parachute?* by Richard Bolles (2003). A summary of college or career offices and nonprofit or commercial career offices can be found online at the What Color Is Your Parachute website, www.jobhuntersbible.com.

CAREER COACHES

According to the Career Coach Institute (www.career-coachinstitute.com), a career coach is simply someone who guides others through job and career changes, helps individuals experience fulfillment in their work, and facilitates the match between employee and job function within a company to optimize his or her contribution and satisfaction.

The career coach's primary role is to serve as a catalyst for transformation and change in the client's work life. Whether the client is at a crossroads of identity and purpose, or just seeking to enrich his or her current work experience, career coaches serve as a guide to the next step in the individual's professional development. Using a respectful, compassionate, yet results-oriented approach, the coach helps his or her clients identify what they most love to do. The next step is to facilitate the client's process in creating that job, career or business. The coach's toolbox includes probing questions, testing of assumptions, standardized assessments, feedback, and other powerful tools as appropriate to the client's unique needs.

As with career counselors, there are very good career coaches and there are some who are new and inexperienced. Look for credentials and experience, and ask for references and a clear outline of the steps that you will take in the process. Some firms, such as AK Consulting Services (www.akAcademy.com, 978-779-6356), specialize in working with both parents and their children. Like most coaches, they work on the full range of the career planning process, from self-assessment through job search and résumé writing.

Though many career coaches do have a counseling background, the primary difference between a coach and a counselor is the depth of the counseling and credentials. Good career coaches have a structured process that includes self-assessment instruments, and they should be up to date on all labor market information and job search techniques.

FIRMS THAT SPECIALIZE IN TESTING, INCLUDING APTITUDE, INTEREST, AND PERSONALITY TESTING

One of the firms that specialize in aptitude testing is the Johnson O'Connor Research Foundation (617-536-0409). With testing centers in many major cities, the firm targets its testing for individuals aged fourteen and up who fall into the following categories:

- High school students deciding on a college and major

- College students debating about majors or deciding what types of jobs or graduate programs to apply for in the future

- Students having difficulty in school or with test taking

- Adult professionals making midlife career changes or seeking to fine-tune their chosen career paths

- Women reentering the job market and/or returning to college after children are in school or as children leave home

Firms like Johnson O'Connor "seek to identify where each person's innate abilities lie, and suggest the types of careers and courses in which that person is most likely to find success and satisfaction. In some cases, the scores can shed light on school difficulties or boredom. They can help a student choose the type of college (e.g., small versus large, liberal arts versus technical school) that will suit his or her aptitudes. For adults, the information may help in decisions regarding promotions, changes within a field, shifts to new career directions, and continuing education. In all cases, our goal is to identify the types of tasks and careers for which the person is most naturally suited, with the basic philosophy that people are happiest doing what they do best" (Sandra Larson, director, Johnson O'Connor Research Foundation, Inc.).

An example of firms that do a broader array of testing is Powell & Wagner Associates in Cambridge, Massachusetts (617-494-1650).

The clients may come to us because their parents want a general evaluation of their child's cognitive, emotional, and social growth. Or, they may be seeking guidance in the selection of a suitable secondary school, college, or vocational school. We also evaluate individuals with more serious educational and/or psychological problems. Usually, these will include measures of intellectual function, academic ability, and achievement, as well as personality measures. When necessary, we may administer more extensive projective personality testing, vocational interest tests, aptitude measures, or tests for specific disabilities that may be interfering with the student's performance. The test battery generally requires two days to complete. The recommendations may include such things as the selection of a school, grade placement, tutoring, counseling, or suggest specific resources—e.g., a school, a tutor, a therapist.

> Dr. Douglas H. Powell, psychologist at the Harvard University Health Services, author of *Teenagers: When to Worry and What to Do: Understanding Human Adjustment and Profiles in Cognitive Aging,* and principal author of *MicroCog: Assessment of Cognitive Functioning,* a computerized neuropsychological test.

Evaluation of school-age young people and older individuals is a specialty. After an evaluation, the results are discussed in detail and in person with the individual, as well as with family or appropriate others. This work can include assessment of apparently capable youngsters who may be having trouble in school or elsewhere; school, college, and career counseling; diagnostic evaluations of unusually complex or challenging problems; assessment of learning disabilities and attention deficit disorders; and evaluation research.

The College Board (212-713-8000, www.collegeboard.com), is a national nonprofit membership association whose mission is to prepare, inspire, and connect students to college success and opportunity. They specialize in preparing students for the SAT®, the PSAT/NMSQT®, and the Advanced Placement Program® (AP®).

FIRMS AND RESOURCES THAT SPECIALIZE IN JOB SEARCH AND RECRUITING

One of the best-known resources for the job search process is Richard Bolles's book *What Color Is Your Parachute?*, in which he suggests that the traditional job search methods of mailing out résumés and searching through newspaper ads are the least effective means of finding a job. His research confirms the process we have been advocating. According to Bolles, the keys to successful job hunting are

> doing homework on yourself, to figure out what your favorite and best skills are; then doing face-to-face interviewing for information only, at organizations in your field; followed up by using your personal contacts to get in to see the person-who-actually-has-the-power-to-hire-you (not necessarily the human resources department), and...identifying fields that interest you, then calling employers in those fields to see if they're hiring for the kind of work you can do.

> Richard Bolles, ("The 14 Ways to Look for a Job," *What Color Is Your Parachute?* column, San Francisco *Chronicle & Examiner*, January 17, 1999)

One of his fourteen ways, albeit one of the less effective in his view, is the use of employment agencies, recruiters, or "headhunters" to help your adult children find work. His point is that the self-assessment process is the most important step—knowing what you want and what you have to offer—rather than going after what is being advertised or offered. However, there are some advantages to using a recruiting firm, a reputable one that is able to help people with their job search. This will be especially helpful to your adult children who have worked their way to a position of responsibility only to have lost their job because of a layoff.

According to the Society for Human Resource Management, there are two types of corporate search firms—contingency and retained—both of whom are paid by the company, not the individual searching for work (Claybrook 2000).

- Contingency firms operate on a fee-per-hire basis. That is, they don't receive their fee until an employer hires a candidate they have referred.

- A retained firm is paid a retainer and receives that fee regardless of the ultimate results of a search. Retained recruiters tend to be more concerned with making sure the recruiting process is thorough and appropriate and that the best candidates are presented.

The advantage of using a search firm is that it puts other people on the lookout for opportunities. As long as your child has done the "homework" of self-assessment and exploring options, a recruiter can help him or her find specific openings. It is in the recruiter's best interest to find a good fit, and it costs the candidate nothing (if they charge a fee, go elsewhere, as it is typically the employer that pays the fee.)

There are several potential disadvantages to using a recruiter, however.

- Some employers that may be of interest won't consider hiring through a search firm, and alliance with one may lose opportunities rather than solicit them. Some firms are more reputable than others, and getting aligned with the wrong one can be detrimental. Especially for higher-level jobs, look for recruiters that are certified by the National Association of Executive Recruiters (www.naer.org).

- Some people get locked into the belief that their job search is the responsibility of the search firm, and they fail to do the important work that only they can do. Using an employment service can be one of several strategies—not the only one. The job seeker must know the type of work that fits his interests, skills, and values. And it is up to the job seeker to get the job—recruiters can only get him in the door.

- Beware of recruiting databases that put résumés at the bottom of large piles. The Recruiter Network (www.therecruiternetwork.com) allows job seekers to post their résumé to their database or send it directly to thousands of targeted recruiters.

There are many books and resources available that outline job search strategies. A few of the ones available from www.careerbookstore.com include

Bolles, Richard Nelson (2002). *Job Hunting on the Internet.* Ten Speed Press.

Deluca, Matthew J., and Nanette F. Deluca (2000). *Get a Job in 30 Days or Less: A Realistic Action Plan for Finding the Right Job Fast.* McGraw-Hill Trade.

Graber, Steven (2000). *The Everything Online Job Search Book.* Adams Media Corporation.

Krannich, Ron, and Caryl Krannich (2003). *Job Hunting Guide: Transitioning from College to Career.* Impact Publications.

Liptak, John J. (2002). *Job Search Attitude Inventory.* Provides a quick assessment of how motivated a person is likely to be in finding a job. Jist Publishing.

Riley, Margaret, and Frances E. Roehm (2002). *Guide to Internet Job Searching.* McGraw-Hill/Contemporary Books.

PUBLISHERS OF CAREER-RELATED ASSESSMENTS AND MATERIALS

Numerous organizations provide career development assessments and other resources. Some assessments are available for use without restrictions or academic requirements, while others require administration by practitioners with certain specific credentials and may best be obtained through a guidance or career counselor. A few of these are listed here with a sampling of their instruments or other resources. For a complete catalog, contact each directly at the number provided.

- **CPP, Inc. (formerly Consulting Psychologists Press, Inc.)**
  800-624-1765   **www.cpp.com**

CPP, Inc., publishes the *Strong Interest Inventory* and *Myers-Briggs Type Indicator* (MBTI) instruments as well as a variety of other career-related tests and materials.

Davies-Black® Publishing (an imprint of CPP, Inc.), at the same number, publishes books on career and personality development, including *Real People, Real Jobs* and *Starting Out, Starting Over,* and books explaining the MBTI assessment such as *Are You My Type?*

1. *Strong Interest Inventory* instrument

   Written at the eighth-grade reading level, the *Strong* assessment compares your interests with the interests of happily employed people in 100+ occupations. It is usually offered to high school and college students as they select academic courses and begin to explore the world of work.

2. *Myers-Briggs Type Indicator* (MBTI) instrument

   Written at the eighth-grade reading level (see Chapter 4 of this book).

3. FIRO-B® and FIRO®-BC (for children) instruments

   Measure expressed and wanted levels of inclusion, control, and affection.

4. *Career Beliefs Inventory* (CBI)

For eighth-grade students and older. Useful for planning a career, choosing a college major, expanding career options.

- **Psychological Assessment Resources, Inc. (PAR)**
  813.968.3003 or   **www.parinc.com**
  800-331-8378

  Publishes testing products, books, journals, and other materials in the fields of psychology, counseling, education, health care, business and industry. PAR is the publisher of the *Self-Directed Search* developed by Dr. John Holland, whose theory of careers—(Realistic, Investigative, Artistic, Social, Enterprising, and Conventional)—is noted in Chapter 4. The "RIASEC" model is the basis for many other career inventories used today. The SDS has a youth version, the *SDS Career Explorer*, accessible online. We continue to recommend using online tools only in conjunction with discussions and other methods.

- **AGS Publishing**
  800-624-1765   **www.agsnet.com**

  Publishes the *Harrington-O'Shea Career Decision-Making System*, which offers the ability to assess abilities, interests, and work values all in one instrument. There are two versions available, one for middle school age and one for high school age.

- **Career/LifeSkills Resources**
  877-680-0200   **www.career-lifeskills.com**

  Specializes in tools for personal, professional, counseling, and organization development including the *Myers-Briggs Type Indicator, Strong Interest Inventory*, and FIRO-B instruments, as well as COPSystem and True Colors. They also support these tools with professional training programs and workshops, a guaranteed 48-hour turn-around scoring service, and a complete range of specially selected print and assessment resources.

- **Career Trainer**
  800-888-4945   www.careertrainer.com

  Provides a wide range of career assessments, including card sorts.

- **Career Communications Incorporated**
  800-346-1848   www.careerbookstore.com

  Offers a full line of career success books, workbooks, assessments and videos geared toward both adults and high school/college age students.

- **Career Research and Testing**
  800-888-4945   408-559-4945

  Publishes a comprehensive catalog of books, videotapes, audiotapes, and software on career topics including résumé writing, interview skills, job search, networking, etc. Also publishes several assessment instruments, including card sort assessments of skills, values, and interests.

- **Harvard University Office of Career Services**
  617-495-2595   408-559-4945

  Excellent guides under $15 each to careers in law, government and politics, consulting, investment banking, medicine, and international careers as well as a general guide to career development and the changing job market.

- **Career Press**   201-848-0310

  Numerous publications on interviewing, résumé writing, and job hunting.

- **National Association of Colleges and Employers**
  800-544-5272, ext. 28   www.naceweb.org

  Offers numerous books on career planning, global workforce, diversity, interviewing, etc.

- **National Society for Experiential Education**
  919-787-3263   www.nsee.org

  Offers excellent and comprehensive directories of internships.

- **Pearson Assessments**
  800-622-7271, ext. 5137   www.pearsonassessments.com

  Publishers of the *Campbell Interest and Skill Survey* (CISS).

- **Peterson's**
  609-243-9111, ext. 224   www.petersons.com

  Offers books on internships and the "hidden job market."

JOB SEARCH AND CAREER SERVICES ON THE INTERNET

Online career resources include interest groups/clubs/forums, career counseling, and bulletin boards. Below are some addresses that include career-related information.

America's Job Bank	www.ajb.dni.us
CareerBuilder.com	www.careerbuilder.com
CareerMag.com	www.careermag.com
Careers.Org	www.careers.org
Dice (Tech Jobs, Tech Talent)	www.dice.com
FinAid (Financial Aid)	www.finaid.org
FlipDog	www.flipdog.com
Help Wanted–USA	iccweb.com
Hot Jobs	www.hotjobs.com
Job Corps Career Development Resource Center	www.jccdrc.org
Job-Hunt	www.job-hunt.org
JobStar, job search guide (public library sponsored)	www.jobsmart.org
Monster	www.monster.com
MonsterTRAK	www.jobtrak.com
NationJob Network	www.nationjob.com
Peterson's	www.petersons.com
The Riley Guide	www.rileyguide.com
Shepp Design	www.Sheppdesign.com/jobsearch.htm

Triumph College Admissions	www.testprep.com
US Department of Education	www.ed.gov
US Employment & Training	www.doleta.gov
WorkTree.com	www.worktree.com

ADDITIONAL PRINT MATERIALS

A wide variety of written material is available to help with the career discovery process. In addition to the previous summary listing resources by age appropriateness, we offer here a select bibliography of additional books and articles on self-assessment, career options, job search and résumé preparation, the changing world of work, and general parenting, as well as some of the career theory research that is foundational to our overall approach and recommendations. The listing is meant to give you a sample of the kinds of materials available. For more information on career guidance materials, consult your library, career center, or online text identification system.

SELF-ASSESSMENT

Bolles, Richard Nelson (2003). *What Color Is Your Parachute? 2003: A Practical Manual for Job-Hunters and Career Changers.* Berkeley, CA: Ten Speed Press.

Carney, Clarke G., and Dina F. Wells (1998). *Working Well, Living Well: Discover the Career Within You* (5th ed.). Stamford, CT: Wadsworth.

Dunning, Donna (2001). *What's Your Type of Career? Unlock the Secrets of Your Personality to Find Your Perfect Career Path.* Palo Alto, CA : Davies-Black Publishing.

Fellman, Wilma R. (2000). *Finding a Career That Works for You: A Step-by-Step Guide to Choosing a Career and Finding a Job.* Chicago: Independent Publishers Group.

Gale, Linda (1998). *Discover What You're Best At* (Rev. ed.). New York: Fireside.

Gardner, Howard (1993). *Multiple Intelligences.* New York: Basic Books.

Hammer, Allen L. (1993). *Introduction to Type® and Careers.* Palo Alto, CA: CPP, Inc.

Janson, Julia (2003). *I Don't Know What I Want But I Know It's Not This: A Step-by-Step Guide to Finding Gratifying Work*. New York: Penguin USA.

Keirsey, David, and Marilyn Bates (1998). *Please Understand Me: Character and Temperament Types* (6th ed.). Del Mar, CA: Promethean Nemesis.

Kelley, Robert E. (1999). *How to Be a Star at Work*. New York: Three Rivers Press.

Kroeger, Otto, and Janet M. Thuesen (2002). *Type Talk at Work*. New York: Delacorte Press.

Lock, Robert D. (1997). *Taking Charge of Your Career Direction: Career Planning Guide: Book I, Book II, Student Activities* (3rd ed.). Pacific Grove, CA: Brooks/Cole.

Lore, Nicholas (1998). *The Pathfinder: How to Choose or Change Your Career for a Lifetime of Satisfaction and Success*. New York: Fireside.

Murphy, Elizabeth (1993). *The Developing Child: Using Jungian Type to Understand Children*. Palo Alto, CA: Davies-Black Publishing.

Myers, Isabel Briggs, with Peter B. Myers (1995). *Gifts Differing: Understanding Personality Type*. Palo Alto, CA: Davies-Black Publishing.

Peterson, Linda (1995). *Starting Out, Starting Over: Finding the Work That's Waiting for You*. Palo Alto, CA: Davies-Black Publishing.

Ryan, Robin (2002). *What to Do with the Rest of Your Life : America's Top Career Coach Shows You How to Find or Create the Job You'll LOVE*. New York: Fireside.

Simonsen, Peggy (2000). *Career Compass: Navigating Your Career Strategically in the New Century*. Palo Alto, CA: Davies-Black Publishing.

Tieger, Paul D., and Barbara Barron-Tieger (1992). *Do What You Are: Discover the Perfect Career for You Through the Secrets of Personality Type.* Boston: Little, Brown.

Van Gelder, Lawrence (1996, Jan. 7.). "Remembering all the roads not taken." *New York Times.*

Whitely, Richard C. (2001). *Love the Work You're With.* New York: Henry Holt & Co.

Wirths, Claudine G., and Mary Bowman-Druhm (1992). *Are You My Type?* Palo Alto, CA: Davies-Black Publishing.

CAREER OPTIONS

Davis, Barbara Kerr, and Barry Sommer (1992). *You Can Choose Your Own Life: A Decision-Making Program for Students.* Palo Alto, CA: Davies-Black Publishing.

Farr, Michael (forthcoming). *Best Jobs for the 21st Century* (3rd ed.). Indianapolis, IN: Jist Works.

Harr, Gary Lynn (1995). *Career Guide: Road Maps to Meaning in the World of Work.* Pacific Grove, CA: Brooks/Cole.

Lindsay, Norene (forthcoming). *Dream Catchers: Developing Career and Educational Awareness* (3rd ed.). Indianapolis, IN: Jist Works.

Lindsay, Norene (forthcoming). *Dream Catchers Activities: Career Development Activities* (3rd ed.). Indianapolis, IN: Jist Works.

Montross, David H., Zandy B. Leibowitz, and Christopher J. Shinkman (1995). *Real People, Real Jobs.* Palo Alto, CA: Davies-Black Publishing.

Occupational Outlook Handbook (2002–2003). U.S. Department of Labor, available through Psychological Assessment Resources, Inc. (800-331-TEST). Updated every two years.

GOAL SETTING

Campbell, David P. (1994). *If You Don't Know Where You're Going, You'll Probably End Up Somewhere Else.* New York: Tabor.

Waitley, Denis (1996). *The New Dynamics of Goal Setting: Flex Tactics for a Fast Changing World.* New York: Morrow.

JOB HUNTING, RÉSUMÉ WRITING, INTERVIEWING

Baber, Anne, and Lynne Waymon (2001). *Make Your Contacts Count: Networking Know-How for Cash, Clients, and Career Success.* New York: AMACOM.

Claybrook, Tracy (2000). "Recruiters are the marketers." *Employment Management Today,* 5(3).

Crispin, Gerry, and Mark Mehler (2003). *CareerXroads 2003* (8th ed.). MMCgroup.

Dike, L, Margaret Riley, Frances Roehm, and Public Library Association (2002). *Guide to Job Searching, 2002–2003.* Blacklick, OH: McGraw-Hill Contemporary Books.

Enelow, Wendy S. (2002). *101 Ways to Recession-Proof Your Career.* Indianapolis, IN: Jist Works.

Enelow, Wendy S., and Louise M. Kursmark (2001). *Expert Resumes for Computer and Web Jobs.* Indianapolis, IN: Jist Works.

Fry, Ron (2003). *101 Smart Questions to Ask on Your Interview.* Franklin Lakes, NJ: Career Press.

Fry, Ron (2002). *101 Great Resumes* (Rev. ed.). Franklin Lakes, NJ: Career Press.

Fry, Ron (2000). *101 Great Answers to the Toughest Interview Questions* (4th ed.). Franklin Lakes, NJ: Career Press.

Hansen, Katharine (2000). *A Foot in the Door: Networking Your Way into the Hidden Job Market.* Berkeley, CA: Ten Speed Press.

Jist Editors (2003). *Creating Your High School Portfolio: An Interactive Guide for Documenting and Planning Your Education, Career, and Life.* Indianapolis, IN: Jist Works.

Kennedy, Joyce Lain (2002). *Resumes for Dummies* (4th ed.). Indianapolis, IN: Wiley.

Kennedy, Joyce Lain (2000). *Job Interviews for Dummies* (2nd ed.). Indianapolis, IN: Wiley.

Noble, David F. (2000). *Gallery of Best Resumes: A Special Collection of Quality Resumes by Professional Resume Writers* (2nd ed.). Indianapolis, IN: Jist Works.

Parker, Yana (2002). *The Damn Good Resume Guide* (4th ed.). Berkeley, CA: Ten Speed Press.

Parker, Yana (1996). *The Resume Catalog: 200 Damn Good Examples* (Updated ed.). Berkeley, CA: Ten Speed Press.

Troutman, Kathryn Kraemer (2003). *Creating Your High School Resume: A Step-by-Step Guide to Preparing an Effective Resume for Jobs, College, and Training Programs.* Indianapolis IN: Jist Works

Weddle, Peter (2003). *Weddle's Job Seeker's Guide to Employment Web Sites* (4th ed.). Stamford, CT: Weddle's.

Yates, Martin (2003). *Knock 'Em Dead.* Avon, MA: Adams Media Corp.

RECENT GRADUATES

Bardwell, Chris (2003). "Making the transition from college to the world of work." *Black Collegian Online,* www.black-collegian.com.

Holton, Elwood R., and Sharon S. Naquin (2001). *How to Succeed in Your First Job: Tips for New College Graduates.* San Francisco: Berrett-Koehler.

McBride, Pamela M. (2003). "From campus to corporate life: Strategies to succeed." *Black Collegian Online,* www.black-collegian.com.

Phifer, Paul (2003). *College Majors and Careers: A Resource Guide for Effective Life Planning* (5th ed.). Chicago: Ferguson.

THE CHANGING WORLD OF WORK

Bridges, William (2003). *Managing Transitions: Making the Most of Change.* Reading, MA: Addison-Wesley.

Bridges, William (1998). *Creating You & Company: Learn to Think Like the CEO of Your Career.* Reading, MA: Addison-Wesley.

Dent, Harry S. (1999). *Job Shock: Four New Principles Transforming Our Work and Business.* New York: St. Martin's Press.

Hakim, Cliff (2003). *We Are All Self-Employed: A New Social Contract Affecting Every Worker and Organization.* San Francisco: Berrett-Koehler.

Hakim, Cliff (1993). *When You Lose Your Job: Laid Off, Fired, Early Retired, Relocated, Demoted, Unchallenged.* San Francisco: Berrett-Koehler.

Kaye, Beverly, and Sharon Jordan-Evans (2003). *Love It, Don't Leave It: 26 Ways to Get What You Want at Work.* San Francisco: Berrett-Koehler.

Kotter, John P. (1995). *The New Rules: How to Succeed in Today's Post-Corporate World.* New York: Free Press.

Montross, David H., and Shinkman, Christopher J., (1996). "Which world are we preparing students for?" Keynote address, ECEN Fall Conference, Falmouth, MA.

Moses, Barbara (1998). *Career Intelligence: The 12 New Rules for Work and Life Success.* San Francisco: Berrett-Koehler.

Noer, David M. (1995). *Healing The Wounds: Overcoming the Trauma of Layoffs and Revitalizing Downsized Organizations.* San Francisco: Jossey-Bass.

Reich, Robert B. (2001). *The Future of Success: Working and Living in the New Economy.* New York: Knopf.

Reinhold, Barbara B. (2001). *Free to Succeed: Designing the Life You Want in the New Free Agent Economy.* New York: Dutton/Plume.

Robinson, Jacquelyn (2003). *Parents Can Help Teens Choose a Career.* Alabama Cooperative Extension System.

Tulgan, Bruce (1998). *Work This Way: How 1000 Young People Designed Their Own Careers in the New Workplace—and How You Can Too.* New York: Hyperion.

Waitley, Dennis (1996). *Empires of the Mind: Lessons to Lead and Succeed in a Knowledge-Based World.* New York: Morrow.

Wright, Dixie Lee (2003). *Job Smarts: 12 Steps to Job Success* (2nd ed.). Indianapolis, IN: Jist Works.

Yates, Martin John (1995). *Beat the Odds: Career Buoyancy Tactics for Today's Turbulent Job Market.* New York: Ballantine Books.

GENERAL BOOKS AND ARTICLES FOR PARENTS

Adolescence Directory On-Line. Indiana University Bloomington School of Education. http://education.indiana.edu/cas/adol.

Begley, Sharon (1996, Feb. 19.). "Your child's brain: How kids are wired for music, math & emotions." *Newsweek.*

Brown, Scott (2003). *How to Negotiate with Kids: 7 Essential Skills To End Conflict and Bring More Joy into Your Family.* New York: Penguin Group.

Carey, A., and S. Parker (1998). "Class of '01 not their parents." *USA Today.*

Clinton, Hillary Rodham (1996). *It Takes a Village*. New York: Random House.

Davison, Alan (1996). *How Good Parents Raise Great Kids: The Six Essential Habits of Highly Successful Parents.* New York: Warner.

Elkind, David (2001). *The Hurried Child: Growing Up Too Fast, Too Soon* (3rd ed.). Reading, MA: Addison-Wesley.

Elkind, David (2000). *All Grown Up and No Place to Go: Teenagers in Crisis* (3rd ed.). Reading, MA: Addison-Wesley.

Eng, Sherri (1996, Oct. 6.). "Parents can help children find the career that fits them best." *Washington Post*.

English, Bella (1996, Aug. 25.). "Fringe benefit: Happier children (research shows that parents happy at work are most likely to have well-adjusted youngsters)." *Boston Globe*.

Evans, Kathy M., Joseph C. Rotter, and Joshua M. Gold (2002). *Synthesizing Family, Career, and Culture: A Model for Counseling in the Twenty-First Century.* Alexandria, VA: American Counseling Association.

Fenwick, Elizabeth, and Tony Smith (1996). *Adolescence: The Survival Guide for Parents and Teenagers.* New York: DK Publishing.

Fleming, Don (1989). *How to Stop the Battle with Your Teenager: A Practical Guide to Solving Everyday Problems.* New York: Simon & Schuster.

Godfrey, Neale S., and Carolina Edwards (1994). *Money Doesn't Grow on Trees: A Parent's Guide to Raising Financially Responsible Children.* New York: Simon & Schuster.

Goleman, Daniel (1995). *Emotional Intelligence*. New York: Bantam Books.

Gray, Kenneth (2000). *Getting Real: Helping Teens Find Their Future*. Thousand Oaks, CA: Corwin Press.

"Great transitions: Preparing adolescents for a new century, concluding report of the Carnegie Council on Adolescent Development" (1995). New York: Carnegie Corporation of New York.

Hurley, Dan, and Jim Thorp (Eds.). (2002). "National study on career guidance and decision-making among American youth." *In Decisions Without Direction: Career Guidance and Decision-Making Among American Youth.* Big Rapids, MI: Ferris State University Career Institute for Education and Workforce Development.

Jacobsen, Mary H. (1999). *Hand-Me-Down Dreams.* New York: Three Rivers Press.

Kitchen, Patricia (2003, June 29). "Kids' job hunt is becoming parents' too." *Tribune Newspapers: Newsday.*

Lancaster, Hal (1996, Feb. 27). "A father's character, not his success, shapes kids' careers." *Wall Street Journal.*

Louv, Richard (2003). *The Superchild Syndrome.* www.connectforkids.org.

Malouff, John, and Nicola Schutte (1998). *Games to Enhance Social and Emotional Skills: Sixty-Six Games That Teach Children, Adolescents and Adults Skills Crucial to Success in Life.* Springfield, IL: Charles C. Thomas.

Melheim, Richard Alan (1996). *101 Ways to Get Your Adult Children to Move Out (and Make Them Think It Was Their Idea).* New York: Doubleday.

Milmore, Donna (1996, June 9). "Job-hunting season gets under way: Specialists offer a few do's and don'ts for parents." *Boston Sunday Globe.*

"Multiple Intelligences explanation and online survey." www.myschoolonline.com.

Otto, Luther B. (1996). *Helping Your Child Choose a Career.* Indianapolis, IN: Jist Works.

Reschke, Wayne, and Karen H. Knierim (1987, Spring). "How parents influence career choice." *Journal of Career Planning and Employment*, 54–60.

Rosenfeld, Alvin, Nicole Wise, and Robert Coles (2001). *The Over-Scheduled Child: Avoiding the Hyper-Parenting Trap.* New York: St. Martin's Press.

Schneider, Barbara, and David Stevenson (1999). *The Ambitious Generation: America's Teenagers, Motivated but Directionless.* New Haven, CT: Yale University Press.

Tabor, Mary B. W. (1996, Aug. 7). "Comprehensive study finds parents and peers are most crucial influences on students." *New York Times.*

Wolf, Anthony E. (1991). *Get Out of My Life, but First Could You Drive Me and Cheryl to the Mall?* New York: Noonday Press.

CAREER RESEARCH AND REFERENCES

Arbona, C. (1995). "Theory and research on racial and ethnic minorities: Hispanic Americans." In F. T. L. Leong (Ed.), *Career Development and Vocational Behavior of Racial and Ethnic Minorities* (pp. 37–66). Mahway, NH: Erlbaum

Arnstein, Robert L. (1984). "Young Adulthood: Stages of Maturity." In D. Offer and M. Sabshin (Eds.), *Normality and the Lifecycle.* New York: Basic Books.

Bandura, A. (1986). *Social Foundations of Thought and Action: A Social Cognitive Theory.* Upper Saddle River, NJ: Prentice Hall.

Barling, J., K. A. Rogers, and E. K. Kelloway (1995). "Some effects of teenagers' part-time employment: The quantity and quality of work make the difference." *Journal of Organizational Behavior, 16,* 143–154.

Bergin, D.A. (1992). "Leisure activity, motivation, and academic achievement in high school students." *Journal of Leisure Research, 24,* 225–239.

Blustein, D. L., L. E. Devenis, and B. A. Kidney (1989). "Relationship between the identity formation process and career development." *Journal of Counseling Psychology, 36,* 196–202.

Brown, M. T. (1995). "The career development of African Americans: Theoretical and empirical issues." In F. T. L. Leong (Ed.), *Career Development and Vocational Behavior of Racial and Ethnic Minorities* (pp. 37–66). Mahwah, NJ: Erlbaum.

Bruner, J. (1988). "After John Dewey, what?" In Kevin Ryan and James M. Cooper (Eds.), *Kaleidoscope: Readings in Education* (5th ed.). Boston: Houghton Mifflin.

Bynner, John M. (1997). "Basic skills in adolescents' occupational preparation." *Career Development Quarterly, 45,* 305–321.

De Meuse, Kenneth P., and Walter W. Tornow (1993). *Leadership and the Changing Psychological Contract Between Employer and Employee.* Greensboro, NC: Center for Creative Leadership.

Didion, Joan (1961). *Slouching Toward Bethlehem.* New York: Noonday Press.

Elkind, David (1994). "Egocentrism in adolescence." *Child Development,* 1026–1033.

Erikson, Erik (1968). *Self and Identity.* New York: W. W. Norton.

Finch, M. D., M. J.Shannahan, J. T. Mortimer, and S. Ryu (1991). "Work experience and control orientation in adolescence." *American Sociological Review, 56,* 597–611.

Gilligan, C. (1982). "New maps of development, new visions of maturity." *American Journal of Orthopsychiatry, 52,* 199–213.

Ginzberg, Eli (1979). *Good Jobs, Bad Jobs, No Jobs.* Washington, DC: University Microfilms.

Herr, Edwin L. (1997). Super's life-span, life-space approach and its outlook for refinement. *Career Development Quarterly, 45,* 238–246.

Holland, John (1997). *Making Vocational Choices* (3rd ed.). Lutz, FL: Psychological Assessment Resources.

Johnson, M. L., J. L Swartz, and W. E. Martin, (1995). "Applications of psychological theories for career development with Native Americans." In F. T. L. Leong (Ed.), *Career Development and Vocational Behavior of Racial and Ethnic Minorities* (pp. 37–66). Mahwah, NJ: Erlbaum.

Jordan, Judith V., Alexandra G. Kaplan, Jean Baker Miller, Irene P. Stiver, and Janet L. Surrey (1991). *Women's Growth in Connection.* New York: Guilford.

Kablaoui, B.N., & Pautler, A.J. (1991). "The effects of part-time work experience on high-school students." *Journal of Career Development, 17,* 195–211.

Kracke, Barbel (1997). Parental behaviors and adolescents' career exploration. *Career Development Quarterly, 45,* 341–350.

Lent, Robert W., and Steven D. Brown (1996). Social cognitive approach to career development: An overview. *Career Development Quarterly, 44,* 310-321.

Lent, Robert W., K. C. Larkin, and S. D. Brown (1989). "Relation of self-efficacy to inventoried vocational interests." *Journal of Vocational Behavior, 34,* 279–288.

Leong, F. T. L., and F.C. Serafica (1995). "Career development of Asian Americans: A research area in need of a good theory." In F. T. L. Leong (Ed.), *Career Development and Vocational Behavior of Racial and Ethnic Minorities* (pp. 37–66). Mahwah, NJ: Erlbaum.

Marcia, J. E. (1980). "Identity in adolescence." In J. Adelson (Ed.), *Handbook of Adolescent Psychology* (pp. 159–187). New York: Wiley.

Meeus, Wim, Maja Dekovic,and Jurjen Iedema (1997). "Unemployment and identity in adolescence: A social comparison perspective. *Career Development Quarterly*, *45*, 369–379.

Montross, David H., and Shinkman, Christopher J. (1992). *Career Development: Theory and Practice.* Springfield, IL: Charles C. Thomas.

Nevill, Dorothy D. (1997). "The development of career development theory." *Career Development Quarterly*, *45*, 288–291.

Noer, David M. (1993). *Leadership in an Age of Layoffs.* Greensboro, NC: Center for Creative Leadership.

Paikoff, R. L., and J. Brooks-Gunn (1990). "Physiological processes: What role do they play during the transition to adolescence?" In R. Montemayer, G. R. Adams, and T. P. Guilota (Eds.), *From Childhood to Adolescence: A Transitional Period.* Newbury Park, CA: Sage.

Phillips, S. D., E. K. Christopher-Sisk, and K. L. Gravino, (2001). "Making career decisions in a relational context." *Counseling Psychologist, 29,* 193–213.

Raskin, Patricia M. (1998). "Career maturity: The construct's validity, vitality, and viability. *Career Development Quarterly, 47,* 32–35.

Savickas, Mark L. (1997). Career adaptability: An integrative construct for life-span, life-space theory. *Career Development Quarterly, 45,* 247–257.

Schmotkin, Dov, and Nitza Eyal (2003, Summer). "Psychological time in later life: Implications for counseling." *Journal of Counseling and Development, 81,* 259–267.

Schultheiss, Donna E. Palladino (2003, Summer). "A relational approach to career counseling: Theortical integration and practical application." *Journal of Counseling & Development, 81* (3), 301–310.

Steinberg, L. (1990). "Autonomy, conflict, and harmony in the family relationship." In S. S. Feldman and G. R. Elliott (Eds.), *At the Threshold: The Developing Adolescent.* Cambridge, MA: Harvard University Press.

Steinberg, L., S. Fegley, and S.M. Dornbusch (1993). "Negative impact of part-time work on adolescent adjustment: Evidence from a longitudinal study." *Developmental Psychology, 29,* 171–180.

Stern, D., and Y. Nakata (1989). "Characteristics of high school students' paid jobs, and employment experience after graduation." In D. Stern and D. Eichorn (Eds.), *Adolescence and Work: Influences of Social Structure, Labor Markets, and Culture* (pp. 189–233). Mahwah, NJ: Erlbaum.

Stern, D., J. Stone, C. Hopkins, and M. McMillon (1990). "Quality of students' work experience and orientation toward work." *Youth and Society, 22,* 263–282.

Sjoberg, L. (1984). "Interests, effort, achievement, and vocational preference." *British Journal of Educational Psychology, 54,* 89–205.

Sjoberg, L. and B. M. Drottz, (1983). "Interests in school subjects and vocational preference." *Scandinavian Journal of Educational Research, 27,* 165–182.

Skorikov, Vladimir B., and Fred W. Vondracek (1997). "Longitudinal relationship between part-time work and career development in adolescents." *Career Development Quarterly, 3,* 221–233.

Super, D. E., M. L. Savickas, and C. M. Super (1996). "The life-span, life-space approach to careers." In D. Brown, L. Brooks, and Associates (Eds.), *Career Choice and*

Development (3rd ed., pp. 2121–2178). San Francisco: Jossey-Bass.

Super, Donald E., Branimir Sverko (Eds.), with Charles M. Super (1995). *Life Roles, Values, and Careers: International Findings of the Work Importance Study.* San Francisco: Jossey-Bass.

Swanson, J. L. (1992). "Vocational behavior, 1989–1991: Life-span career development and reciprocal interaction of work and nonwork." *Journal of Vocational Behavior, 41,* 101–161.

Vondracek, F. W. (1995). "Promoting vocational development in early adolescence. In R.M. Lerner (Ed.), *Early adolescence: Perspectives on research, policy, and intervention* (pp. 277-292) Mahwah, NJ: Erlbaum.

Vondracek, Fred W. and Matthias Reitzle (1998). "The viability of career maturity theory: A developmental-contextual perspective." *Career Development Quarterly, 47,* 6–15.

Vondracek, Fred W., and Vladimir B. Skorikov (1997). "Leisure, school and work activity preferences and their role in vocational identity development." *Career Development Quarterly, 45,* 322-340.

White, Burton L. (1994, May). "Head start: Too little and too late. How a child develops in the first three years of life often determines success or failure in school." *Principal,* pp. 13–15.

Young, Richard A. (1994). "Helping adolescents with career development: The active role of parents." *Career Development Quarterly, 42,* 195–203.

INDEX

A

action plans, 100

action taking: motivation and, 76, 108–109; Motivator role in, 49; by parents, 26–31; by preschool child, 186; by school-age child, 191; by teenagers, 197; by young adults, 202–203

adolescence: early (ages twelve to fourteen). *See* early adolescence (ages twelve to fourteen); later (ages fifteen to seventeen). *See* later adolescence (ages fifteen to seventeen); nature of, 148–149; self-identity established in, 148; stages of, 147; transitional nature of, 148–149. *See also* teenagers

adolescent(s): aptitude testing of, 227; search for identity by, 6; variations in, 147–148. *See also* teenagers

adolescent egocentrism, 149

adulthood: career coaching in, 201–205; later (ages twenty-two and over). *See* later adulthood (ages twenty-two and over); young (ages eighteen to twenty-two). *See* young adulthood (ages eighteen to twenty-two)

adventure: encouraging of, 138; values of, 64

aesthetic values, 64

aggressiveness, 71

alumni networks, 219

apathy, 108–109

aptitude testing, 227

artistic type, of person, 56

aspirations: description of, 5; of parents, 29–30

assessments: career-related, 232–235; self-assessments. *See* self-assessment

B

baby boomers, 37–38

Bandura, Albert, 150–151

Bolles, Richard, 229

C

Campbell, David, 96

Campbell, Joseph, 69

Campbell Interest and Skill Survey, 218

career: adaptability of, 24; advice regarding, 8; assumptions regarding, 11–13; case studies of, 11; child's vs. parent's, 9–10; definition of, 21; discouraging of, 106; exploration of, 76–77; information sources regarding, 80–81, 84; materials for, 232–235; modern-day choices for, 98–99; motivators for, 55–56; of parent. *See* parental career; personal nature of, 99; reading about, 80–81; research resources, 247–252; static, 52; transitions in, 125–127; trends in, 41; twentieth-century structure of, 59; vision of, 126; vulnerability of, 91. *See also* job search; work

Career Beliefs Inventory, 233

career coach, 225–226

career coaching: in adulthood, 201–205; benefits of, 6; characteristics of, 16; definition of, 6–9, 45; of preschool child, 185–187; of school-age child, 190–192; of teenagers, 195–198; understanding of, 7–9

career coaching firms: aptitude testing, 227; description of, 226, 227–229; job search, 229–231

career counseling, 218

career counselor: credentials of, 223; ethical practices by, 224–225; fees, 224; how to find, 224–225; roles of, 222–223; services provided by, 223; training of, 223

career decision making: challenges associated with, xi–xii; description of, 176; focus of, 98; influences on, 30, 32; motivations for, 109–110; nonlinear nature of, 51; ongoing nature of, 37;

parental involvement in, xiv, 13; process of, 51–52; rewards of, 107

career decision-making model: diagram of, 20; goal setting and planning. *See* goal setting; options for career. *See* career exploration; self-assessment stage. *See* self-assessment

career development assessments and materials, 232–235

career exploration: and college, 78–79; considerations for, 175–177; data-gathering approaches, 77; Internet resources, 180–181; long-term employment, 85–86; overview of, 75; for preschool child, 185; resources for, 177–180; for school-age child, 190; self-assessments matched to, 76–78; self-awareness benefits of, 93; short-duration employment and courses for, 84–85; for teenagers, 195–196; tentative substage of, 158

career fairs, 219

career fields: description of, 80; learning about, 80–86; networking about, 81–84

career growth, 85

career library, 220

career options: eliminating of, 110; resources for, 240; self-assessments matched to, 76–78

career planning: changes in, 24; computer-based systems for, 208–210, 218–219; in early adolescence, 151–152; in early childhood, 137–138; historical view of, 24; in late childhood, 141, 143; in later adulthood, 171–172; "life-space" approach, 39; in young adulthood, 167–168

career satisfaction: of parents, 21; sources of, 53–57

career services: college-based, 113–115, 218–221; computer-based career planning systems, 208–210; guidance counselors, 158, 208; for high